"Only You Can Save Yourself"

~ Shrimad Bhagwad Gita ~

First published in 2017 by

Becomeshakespeare.com
Wordit Content Design & Editing Services Pvt Ltd
Unit - 26, Building A-1, Nr Wadala RTO,
Wadala (East),
Mumbai 400037, India
T:+91 8080226699

Copyright © 2017 by Vikas Trivedi
All rights reserved. Any unauthorized reprint or use of this material is prohibited. No part of this book may be reproduced or transmitted in any form or by any means, electronic or mechanical, including photocopying, recording, or by any information storage and retrieval system without express written permission from the author/publisher.

Please do not participate in or encourage piracy of copyrighted materials in violation of the author's rights. Purchase only authorized editions.

©
ISBN: 978-93-86487-45-2

A teacher of English and Psychology, Vikas Trivedi holds Master Degrees in English Literature, Political Science and Psychology. He is born on December 2nd, 1991 in Dungarpur, Rajasthan and is currently pursuing his PhD. Despite having failed in English due to difficulty in grasping, he had turned his weakness into his strength and grown up to study the language and now, teach it.

Vikas Trivedi believes in the law of attraction and in magic of making the impossible into possible by his strength, positivity and motivation. He loves to read and has a vast collection of books. He also loves to listen to music as well as travelling.

With this book, Vikas Trivedi hopes to reach out to maximum number of people and be the guiding source in assisting them deal with each and every, small and big problem life throws at them. The book has been written after years of research and study, with the view that every single reader can find their hidden spark.

Connect with Vikas:

 vikas.trivedi.543    www.vikastrivedi.in

 vikas786trivedi@gmail.com    vikastrivedivikku

"Rich People focus on Richness and Vitality whereas Poor People focus on Poverty and Adjustment"

~ Vikas Trivedi ~

Acknowledgement

My beloved friends, Namaste! I am Vikas Trivedi from Rajasthan, India. By profession, I am a teacher. I love to study, write and spread knowledge. I think the urge to spread knowledge comes from the fact that I used to be a poor student, so much that there was a time when I had thought of dropping out of school after failing in English. The episode hit me so hard that I decided to turn it in my favour and now I have become a teacher of English and Psychology.

I have read and heard people telling that think positive, stay cool, work hard, use the law of attraction, feel good, God be with you etc... but I have always question to ask that how ?? How can we think positive, how can we stay strong, how long can we work hard, how can we use the law of attraction, how can we feel good, how can we make sure that God is with us?? But I discovered all the answers by myself in this book.

This practical book is a result of thoughts of the great mentors of the world. It is said that one mind has more power than millions cells but when it comes about ten most intelligent and active minds, you can make out how important each word of this book is! I have used my Psychology study to deal with each and every kind of minor and major problems which seem to be difficult for you. I started with rich and successful people to know the hidden secret behind their prosperity. I also started reading the most selling and renowned books to get the more ideas about being a best version of ourselves which have been presented in the practical book.

This book couldn't have been possible without the most talented mentors from the different countries. I am eternally thankful to all of them.

Smita Agarwal is the co-writer of this book. A very interesting fact about her is that she is a noted Pranic Healer. Her knowledge about Pranic Healing and spirituality has made this book helpful and practical.

Rosie Segger from Germany is an expert at using The Law Of Attraction. She has saved millions of people's dreams from failing by exploring the awareness about The Law Of Attraction.

Karen Sullivan form Chicago has left no stone unturned to introduce the most important but difficult seven laws of the universe. I had assigned this tougher task to her to do but she made it so comprehensive by her knowledge.

Pet El Rosch from Germany has showcased the most unbeatable techniques to solve family and business problems.

Hiral Thakkar from India had brought the most interesting and unbelievable sessions about 'Switchwords' with Nishita Jaiswal.

Dr. Nora Kohali, a renowned psychiatrist, from Thailand had played a sparking role in my book. She blessed us by introducing some therapies.

Cora Boham from Germany and Chloe Larissa from Connecticut, have also played important roles as motivational speakers and touched everyone's heart with their exceptional embodies.

Vanessa B Bautista who has a strong background in psychology has prepared a couple of sections in the book which makes the reading more interesting.

Maureen Messier, from New York has put her real life examples in this book which has helped the reading experience more comprehensive.

The rest of my thanks goes to my editor Samarpita Mukherjee Sharma for making this book more readable.

Before writing this book, my entire team and I started a workshop where we got a small stage to put up our unpolished knowledge. As more time went by, the more fruitful the workshop became. We started receiving great feedbacks from all over the world, this idea to put forward this knowledge to the world, was planted in our minds which you are reading right now.

In the end, I would like to thank my family for their regular support as without their guidance this project would have never been possible.

Thank you so much!

Yours faithfully

Vikas Trivedi

Co-Author

Smita Agarwal was born and brought up in Kolkata, India in a middle class family, close knit family with lots of family values. Smita has been a shy and introvert as being youngest in the family she had been bullied at lot by siblings. She grew up with bunch of close friends she made throughout her school life. Was always average in studies but always inquisitive for creative work. Smita is graduate in Accountancy hons. After that, her creativity lead her into interior designing n she did diploma on computer aided designing. After her son was born, Smita got in touch with Pranic Healing which bought a major transformation in my life. Now it's been 10 years and Smita is a professional Pranic Healer. During this time, Smita developed an interest in reading books and she spent hours reading about different topics including Pranic Healing. That was when she was inspired to come up with this book.

After meeting Vikas, she learnt what law of attraction was all about and its various concepts in his workshop. Writing a book on the basis of workshop taken by him, was Vikas' brainchild and Smita assisted him throughout the process. Smita is passionate about travelling and yoga which also happens to be an essential part of her lifestyle.

Regards

Smita A...

Mrs. Smita Agarwal

Mentor's Bio

The law of attraction is working all the time. Vikas Trivedi's workshop was also a sort of the law of attraction which I attracted. I had been asking the universe how I could guide more people to create the life of their dreams, when the universe answered by tripping me up, literally I fell over and broke my wrist, while it was repairing I spent more time than normal reading face book comments. This is where the synchronicity of events took place after 3 days of being shown Vikas Trivedi. I became compelled to offer my support to him on his latest project. I am so thankful for Vikas Trivedi and his co writer Smita Agarwal for giving me the stage where I not only explored myself but also learned many new things from different mentors from various countries.

I used to use the law of attraction on myself but through this workshop I implemented those teachings on myself to be the great mentor and successfully I have done that. After many years of being depressed I found a new way to be, by changing my thoughts and actions I started to see incredible changes in my life. By sharing this knowledge weekly with the members of this group it has brought me an abundance of happiness and joy in sharing their many successes which they achieved week after week. I am privileged to have been a part of this wonderful journey and I really appreciate the way this book "The Hidden Spark" is prepared. This is a must-read book. It is a great guide.

Regards

Rosie Segger, Spain

Mentor's Bio

We all carry this spark within, sometimes it just needs a little recall using it for us . Exactly that happened during the creation of this book, in such a very special way. Using the power of the hidden spark, uniting several cultures, countries and connecting spiritual knowledge, experienced wisdom combined with helpful applications, mindfulness and gratitude - supporting and reminding each others

Open minded strangers who became friends, enjoying together the miracles that one's own will can accomplish, related following the success of a more and more conscious living connected by the WORLD WIDE WEB .

"The Hidden Spark" a new proof of loving coexistence, mutually respect and positive thinking creates positive feelings creates confident harmony and we are all together in this. I give my big thanks to Vikas Trivedi for involving me in this project because I have learned a great number of things from him and his workshop. I came to know about Indian culture and wisdom of all the mentors. I loved to receive tons of love from the members and I must say that one must read this book "The Hidden Spark" because this is an unbeatable book which presents only practical guidance not theory. Whenever I get stuck somewhere in my life, the teachings of this book is always helpful for me in solving out the problems.

Regards

Pet El Rosch, Germany

Mentor's Bio

Since 1999, I used implementation leadership skills along with certifications in hypnotherapy, life coaching, and NLP modalities to assist clients in gaining awareness, clarity and untapped potential along with an endless list of life possibilities in living a more fulfilled life both personally and professionally, with clarity and intent. As a Certified Law of Attraction Counsellor, I teach my clients how to tap into their own connection to bring about changes on a grand scale in all areas of life. I am the co-author of a new breakthrough in financial awareness module, entering the Prosperity Paradigm© I have authored 2 upcoming books, A Day At A Time, and What If? and is appearing in the upcoming breakout movie and eventual reality show, The Enlightenment Stories as a personal mentor. As far as my mind concerns, I must say that the way all the teachings and chapters are represented in the "The Hidden Spark"; are amazing because the workshop was a stage where we were given a lot of time for the preparations and we always tried our level best to serve the attendees and I feel like my one of the dream has come true after being a part of this excellent workshop which has been run under the observation of the strict and disciplined mentor and author VIkas Trivedi. Thank you so much Vikas Trivedi and co writer Smita Agarwal for involving me in this project.

Regards

Karen Sullivan
Chicago, Illinois, USA

Mentor's Bio

I am a switch word expert. The vital role was assigned to me by Vikas Trivedi for his workshop and the book "The Hidden Spark" as well. I consider myself lucky to be a part of this project. All kinds of people love to use switch words as it is pretty fast giving result if you believe in them. This book is really helpful guide to millions people who are seeking for the correct path in their life. Because this book is a product by many brilliant international mentor's best and practical knowledge. While running the workshop, I found Vikas so friendly with all and dedicated person towards his task. Thank you so much Vikas Trivedi and co writer Smita Agarwal for making me a part of this project.

Regards

Hiral

Hiral Mathuradas Thakkar
Mumbai, India

Mentor's Bio

In the workshop conducted by Vikas Trivedi I explored the concept of switchwords and crystal therapies how they can be used to solve day to day life problems. My experience in this field made a complex topics easily accessible and helped lot of people to achieve their dreams. Vikas tried to cover all the issues in his book " The Hidden Spark" which revolves around the problem regarding money, relationship.education health and manymore.

Regards

Nishita..

Nishita Ashish Jaiswal
Mumbai. India

Mentor's Bio

I am Mexican-American philanthropist, counsellor, inspirational writer and speaker. Graduated from California State University Sacramento with a Bachelors degree in Psychology, then pursued my Masters in Science from the University of Nevada Las Vegas in Clinical Mental Health Counselling. I incorporate Mental and Spiritual interventions in creative outlets such as poetry, speeches, and inspirational messages to empower the human Mind and Spirit. The best thing is that I and Vikas Trivedi both are from the same subject Psychology so it helped me a lot to prepare lectures for the readers. I love the Indian culture since my childhood as I believe in human souls because we are all connected to each other and being guided by the universe. I am so curious person to know new things about the human mind, spirituality, law of attraction, fulfilling dreams in short time, NlPs and many more. Being a human being, I had many doubts but after taking and attending the lecture of the workshop I have filled myself with the tremendous knowledge which guides me in my rest of life as blessings. I found Vikas so focused and disciplined person towards his goal. By making this book "The Hidden Spark" solved the problems of millions people who give up hopes to achieve their goals. This is a wonderful practical guide that leaves you at your correct destination and I am highly impressed by the book "The Hidden Spark". Thank you so much my friend Vikas Trivedi and Smita Agarwal for making me a part of this book.

Regards

Van B.

Vanessa Bazzania Becerra-Bautista
Las Vegas, Nevada, USA

Mentor's Bio

I am an entrepreneur who believes in creating my life as a work of art. I am a life coach and a content strategist for creative entrepreneurs. The Notebook: Become Your Soul Mate Program is based on my transformation process described in this book. I live in upstate New York with my four sons, where you can find me baking, dancing or writing. I love to write and spread the knowledge among the people. The book "The Hidden Spark" uncovers the many secrets of our life. Actually after reading this practical book, you will come to know the hidden power of yours. I would like to suggest all to read this book once as it is made in a way which leaves no doubt for you. I give my enormous gratitude to Vikas Trivedi and co writer Smita Agarwal.

Regards

Maureen Messier
New York

THE HIDDEN SPARK

One spark can....

One book can spark a life,
One idea can play on a fife,
One man can create a history,
One step can solve a mystery.

One word will make your day,
One hope will take on a way,
One spark will be uncovered,
One magic will be discovered.

One has the power to do supreme.
One has the calibre to have extreme,
One has the mind to get at the apex,
One has the potency to write a codex.

(THE HIDDEN SPARK)

Index of the Book

1. MY CHOICE 25
2. FORGIVE YOURSELF 33
3. UNLEARN TO LEARN 39
4. HOW TO MOTIVATE YOURSELF 45
5. REMOVE YOUR MENTAL BLOCKAGES 52
6. THE MAGICAL, "LAW OF ATTRACTION" 59
7. IDENTIFYING THE INTIMATE POWER OF YOU, (THE LAW OF YOU) 69
8. REVERSE PSYCHOLOGY 74
9. GOD'S CALL (A SILENT RING) 81
10. ATTRACTING WEALTH AND MANIFESTING ABUNDANCE . . 89
11. BE A MASTER OF "THE LAW OF ECHO" 103
12. VISUALISATION TO MANIFESTATION 110
13. NO HURRIES FOR THE WORRIES 116
14. FORGET YOUR PAST AND MAKE A MOVE AHEAD 126
15. THE LAW OF KARMA 136
16. SWITCH WORDS. 142
17. AGE IS JUST A NUMBER. 152
18. IMAGINIOTIC THERAPY 159
19. I WAS FOOL BUT NOW I AM FULL 165
20. TIME MANAGEMENT 171
21. HIDDEN BENEFITS OF CRYSTAL 178
22. YOUR QUESTIONS, OUR ANSWERS 182

CHAPTER ONE

My Choice

"The hardest thing to learn in life is which bridge to cross and which to burn."

~ David Russell ~

There was this simpleton who lived in a village. His faith in God bordered on the ridiculous. One day he went to a forest and climbed a tree to pluck some mangoes. In no time, he had scaled the top of the tree in the excitement to pluck as many mangoes as was possible. Suddenly, he saw a snake on a branch near him and he started screaming in fear of the unknown. Some people, including his friends, assembled there to help him by climbing up the tree. Rejecting their offers, the boy said: "Don't bother; God will come to help me."

All those present were shell-shocked. He remained sitting on that branch for some time and in some time; the snake started slithering towards him. People standing below, started to panic. One of his friends, tried to climb the tree again, but was summarily stopped by the boy. The snake kept coming towards him. At last, one old man suggested that he toss the snake with the stick which was tied to his waist. But the boy stubbornly refused any help. Unfortunately, he was soon bitten by the snake and died a little later. After his death, the boy's soul asked God why he did not help his devout disciple. God replied smilingly, "I had offered help in the form of friends, strangers and that stick. You trusted me but did not take advantage of the protective tools offered by me."

Moral of the story is that you should be aware of the choices that are around you and the golden opportunity that can change your life. If you miss it, you have only yourself to blame and nobody else.

I have come across people, in my Money Workshop, who believe in God and have unflinching faith in Him. They are convinced that success is bound to follow if it is in their destiny. This is wishful thinking. Making the effort is the key to success.

Everyone has a choice. I have a choice. You have a choice. We all have choices to make. Choosing something big or small depends on you because this life is gifted by the universe to us. Imagine, that I offer you a big car like BMW or Audi or Mercedes-Benz, what will be your response? Yes, or no. Suppose I offer you a big house or a government job or a big stockpile of cash. What will be your reply? I think you would love to accept it and definitely say YES to me. Why? Because we wish to have these things but we don't have money to purchase. It happens because we have tied ourselves with certain limitations like, *I am not financially stable, My father is not a big businessman, I am too old now to start a new life, I am physically and mentally unprepared, I cannot do this, I don't have money to begin my business, I am not good at studies, What others will think of me,* etc. You have a thousand and valid excuses not to pursue your dreams or live a clichéd life. But you have only one option to fulfil our dream. You have 'The Hidden Spark' within you. You only need to ignite it and convert it into a raging fire. Thereafter, all problems will appear insignificant and the all-important dream will be visible and achievable.

Always remember that *God helps those who help themselves.* You might be the most devout disciple of your beloved God and there is no reason why he wouldn't help you, but be aware that miracles don't happen. It is we who make things happen by our own had work. God can only make the opportunity available to you, but it is you who has to recognise the opportunity and act upon it.

When we talk about *the hidden spark* which exists in all of us, it is this ability to grasp the opportunity and the will to work hard to obtain what we desire. You could have a rich businessman father, but what about after you take over the business? You got the opportunity in the form of a readymade business, but it won't run itself. You have to work hard to not only maintain it but to make it bigger than how you received it. If you don't and just laze around, happy to be rich, very soon all your riches will dwindle and you will end up as a pauper.

Opportunities don't knock at our doorstep repeatedly. It is a hit and miss offer which while many are quick to take up and act upon, some let go off only to regret some time later. Making excuses is the sign of the weak and the strong never make excuses. Irrespective of the situation, if the intent is positive, one is bound to find the opportunity even if the situation is adverse.

So finally, have you decided what exactly you want to do in your life? Are your life goals clear in your mind? If yes, then believe me, you have successfully negotiated the biggest hurdle on your way to success and glory.

First of all, let's break the ice and let me ask you the simple question: "What do you want? What is it that you exactly want? Are you really clear about your goals? Are you really on the way to success? If yes then it's fantastic, if no then this book can show you the way to achieve all major milestones in your life. You might have heard a quote by Swami Vivekananda, "You are the creator of your own destiny". It sounds so good to hear but what does this quote mean? How can you be the creator of your own destiny? By making the choice. Your entire life revolves on the Choice you make. So be very careful while making your choice. Don't hurry! Take your time. I am providing you an Action Plan Form below right here. You are advised to fill it up with a pencil in the book itself after deciding what you exactly want out of your life?

ACTION PLAN FORM

Write your three biggest dreams (Priority wise)

1. _____
2. _____
3. _____

Write your three burning desires

1. _____
2. _____
3. _____

Deadline ® (...)

"A thousand-mile journey begins from a single step". Now you have decided your journey by filling up your dreams. Before going anywhere, you must decide the destination. You have chosen your dreams now and decided to achieve them at any cost. Kindly read your Action Plan Form again and continue reading ahead.

Often, you try your best but you don't channelise efforts in the right direction leading disruptions in the journey to your destination. Here are some points. Kindly read them carefully in order to stay focused on your goals:-

- ➢ Believe that you can do it.
- ➢ Go beyond the limits. Always draw a map for your future because you are the best engineer of your life.
- ➢ Your thoughts matter a lot. Once you have decided to do it make sure you don't look back.
- ➢ Visualise yourself as if you have already achieved your goals and feel like having the victory already in your hands.
- ➢ The environment you create around you will help you stay motivated towards your goal so make sure the things you see, hear, speak, feel, talk are all positive and keep you in the right frame of mind
- ➢ Be a good learner and listener so that you are keen to learn new things in each and every moment.
- ➢ I know that it is quite tough to avoid negative thoughts but the scientists have suggested a way out and want you to divert your mind from it and say to yourself 'Next Please'. The moment you have the thought which makes you feel good is your right zone. Just be in that frequency.

Now about distractions or procrastination which will pull you back and stall your progress. You might have read some motivational books or videos or clips or programmes and found the same idea to stay focused and keep moving to the goals. You might have followed those teachings for some days or weeks or months but do you really stay focused on your goals for a long time? No. Why? It is because you are human being and are tempted to use those things which you enjoy like Smartphones, chatting with friends, playing video games or gossiping. We kill time and then regret at the end of day that we have not done anything important. That's okay. It happens because you are a human being. I am providing you a form again below which will remove blockages from your chosen path:

COMMITMENT FORM
Write five things, which distract you.

1. _____
2. _____
3. _____
4. _____
5. _____

" Every man builds his world in his own image. He has the power to choose, but no power to escape the necessity of choice."

~ Ayn Rand ~

****

REAL PEOPLE, REAL STORIES

Vikas sir and Karen ma'am have really blessed me with health and wealth. In this journey, my life has fully changed and the credit for this goes to them both. I was dealing with lot of issues but both always encouraged me. I have really seen that the law of attraction is workable. 70 per cent of my money issues have solved with amazing experience. My husband had gone through big loss in business over the last two years and now financial miracles have started taking palace. Karen ma'am personally supported me a lot in solving my health issues. She has mentally supported me to overcome my problems. Even my thyroid is absolutely normal now. I am practicing mirror work. I am getting better and better. Vikas sir has changed the way I thought. His psychological tricks worked a lot on me. Now I can say that I am enjoying my life. I suggest everyone to read this book once.

Much Gratitude!

Divya Lamba
Mumbai, India

Hello my friends!! It had been 6 years since I visited my grandparents' place due to some or the other reason. Fortunately, one day while scrolling down my news feed, I saw Vikas sir's post which said people who are interested may inbox him their numbers. Without a second thought, I sent him my contact details. After a few months I was added to the life changing group! So the first session was by Karen Ma'am and she told us to chant "EVERY DAY IN EVERY WAY I'M GETTING BETTER AND BETTER" which I chant daily before going to sleep. Just like this many sessions took place and my imagination power kept on increasing. I kept imaging I'm going there. With my bags all packed. All set to go! I always said I'm going next month. My grand mom a few days back traveled in flight and I kept her ticket safe! Cut her name wrote mine and kept imaging I'm leaving. Three months after joining this group, it finally happened. All thanks to Vikas sir! He has proved to be an angel in many people's lives! He always says, "God bless us", but I'm sure every member in this group prays for him every day – that a person like him should be in everyone's life! After following his money work shop, I invested 2 lakh in plotting business which came back to me with 22 lakh of profit right now. Many thanks to all the mentors!!

Himanshu Bhagchandani
Visakhapatnam, India

CHAPTER TWO

Forgive Yourself

"When you initially forgive, it is like letting go of a hot iron. There is initial pain and the scars will show, but you can start living again."

~ Stephen Richards ~

Right from his childhood, Pradip was a destitute child and begging was the only means of survival for him and his family. Often, they had to skip meals in order to money. For him, going to school was unthinkable and he spent most his time begging for alms to make ends meet. One day he was ruing the loss of a one rupee coin and was crying bitterly outside the bus stand. A pretty lady noticed the boy while she was crossing the road. Moved by the boy's misery, she walked up to him and wanted to know the cause for his pain. He let her know about his incident. The lady felt pity for him and gave him a rupee coin but the boy was inconsolable. He complained that had he not lost the coin earlier he would have two rupees in his kitty. The lady took back her coin from the boy and left in a huff in sheer disgust. Another man offered him a tenner in support. But the repeated the same story and simply refused to learn the lesson that one has to move forward instead of remaining wedded to the past. The man took back the money he had offered to the boy very much like the pretty lady had done earlier even as the boy continued to wail in isolation.

The moral of the story is that if you don't disengage with what had happened in your past then you can't move on in life. Your physical body is like a structure of the vehicle, your mind is said to be an engine but your thoughts work like fuel to keep you going towards your goal. Since in this chapter, we are going to talk about *ForgiveYourself*, I will talk about how your past's mishaps that hold you back. Take a few minutes to muse about your past, to contemplate about your childhood like how your parents or friends treated you, how good or bad you were at studies, how innocent you were, how you missed your chances and how your beloved or loved ones deserted you.

Everyone has a past. The past can be good or bad. The past can be full of good events or mishaps. Your past may be good, like you achieved something big, you scored well in exams, you received a trophy, you got profit in business etc. Your past may be bitter like you failed in exams, you lost your spouse, you separated from your partner, you faced a financial chaos etc. One interesting thing is your past is responsible for your present and your future is fully based on your present. It means if you don't let go your past then be careful because you are attracting the same past in your present and future.

Don't let one failed love, take you off believing in true love. Don't let your poor grades in school, ever convince you that you cannot shine in your work. Remember, that the parameters for those exams were different to the ones your were facing then. You are a different person now, you will excel or fail in your work based on how you act upon it. Same goes for relationships. If one had failed, it does not reflect on the rest of your life and relationships. Leave the past behind, concentrate on what you have in front of you, afresh.

I know that your past may have brought tears into your eyes but I would suggest you let the tears flow. Yes, make your heart light. Don't stop the tears; by doing so you would be only keeping your sorrows within yourself. The trick is to take all sad emotions out of you. Let all negative emotions seep out of your mind and body. Sometimes, even exercising helps. Go for a run, try kickboxing — take the emotions out. And see how light you feel once you have been able to leave the past

The Hidden Spark

behind. This is when you will be ready to embrace the present and the work towards a successful future.

Doesn't matter who you are, what you do and who all know you — always remember that it is okay to cry. If you feel hesitation, tell yourself that this is a great technique that you are using right now. Please stay strong now because here is a form for you to fill up.

In the form below, write down all your mishaps and the dreadful events that have taken place in your life till now. Since we have just revisited the past while reading this chapter, it will now be easy for you to fill the form below.

APOLOGY FORM

Write down about all the sad and upsetting events that have happened in your life, below. Don't be shy or hold yourself back, no one else but you will be seeing the list.

....
....
....
....
....
....
....
....
....
....
....
....
....
....
....
....
....
....

> I, ... (your name) forgive myself for holding deep regrets, depressing thoughts, disappointments, agony, greed, negativity, grudges and arrogant attitude. I declare myself free from the grip of the past mishaps. I have forgiven myself and forgotten everything. I am happy to begin my new life because I am a child of the universe and I deserve the best things in my life. I have become the pure soul. I am on the way to becoming the best version of myself.
>
> Thank you so much.
>
> Date:-   The delighted free person
>
> {...............................}
>
> (Put your name and signature above in the bracket↑)

I congratulate you on making a new beginning. As you have made your choice in the first chapter, about what you exactly want and you have already embarked upon a new journey in just few minutes back in this chapter. I know that you are feeling so fresh and enthusiastic. You have a priceless spark within you which you are not aware of, so this book will help you discover yourself.

"The only person we have the right or the power to forgive is ourselves. For everything else, there is the Art of Acceptance."

~ Rebecca O'Dwyer ~

****

REAL PEOPLE, REAL STORIES

Hello!!. My journey with the law of attraction began when I was nineteen and was introduced to it by a friend. I still remember the sweet memory of that first manifestation that helped me believe the magical power of our thoughts. I am an absolute believer! I was introduced to this group by my good friend Vikas (Vikku, as we all love to call him). I'm so grateful to him for adding me into this lovely group. I absolutely appreciate the efforts, time and abundance of love that the mentors have showered upon us. It has been a phenomenal journey of learning so far! I have changed myself to become a better person. I have stopped procrastinating and believing in the power of present. I learnt the magical power of "Self Love" and the healing power that it has. I have begun to unconditionally love myself more and more. Another beautiful learning experience was learning about "God's call" in a session by Vikku that followed by that session I have started my own blog knowing it's my call to share my insights and to follow my love of writing. I also manifested money as and when I wished by writing down money codes on my wrists as suggested by Mentor Hiral. What a joy it has been to be on the attracting frequency throughout this time. I have become a calmer person and am finding peace by choosing to focus on achieving my goals over worrying. I want to thank you all from the bottom of my heart to our lovely mentors - Vikku, Rosie, Karen, Hiral and Arch tep el rosh, Vanessa, Chloe, Cora, Maureen. Thank you so much for showering your wisdom upon us and spending your valuable time in guiding us to achieve what we're all worth of !

Lots of Love.

Nammy (Namrata Upadhyay)
Kolkata, india

CHAPTER THREE

Unlearn To Learn

The most useful piece of learning for the uses of life is to unlearn what is untrue.

~ Antisthenes ~

A septuagenarian and prosperous farmer with well-defined creases on his forehead found a cute cub on his way back home after a hard day's work. He was a kind man so he took the cub with him. He showered it with his love and affection as he would do for his pet dog. He liberally served the cub bread and milk every day. After a couple of years, that baby grew up to become a lion but the interesting thing was that the lion was *barking* instead of roaring. It had the nature of a dog but the looks of a lion. The moral of this short story is that your mind is shaped by the thoughts which nourish it.

You all are human beings, including me. We are all social animals. Society plays a great role in your life, specially the environment in which you are brought up. Sometimes, it happens that you are unable to energise your powerful mind and actualise your big vision because the place where you live in or the environment you are attached to or the society you belong to, act as countervailing factors to thwart your efforts to outgrow or outshine your peers in life.

Now I talk about the principles which you have learnt in your daily, routine life. These principles and teachings are firmly entrenched in your mental frame. It has almost become your nature which can be equated with orthodox values.

We all know how a newborn has a clean slate for mind. What he is taught, what he observes and what he learns — are what he becomes. The human mind is like a play dough, it can be given different forms in the early stages of life. It is very important to give the correct forms and influence the mind in a positive way. Just like a cub was brought up with dogs and was led to believe that the barking sound is what it needs to make, similarly, children grow up with values we teach them.

We must also not forget that nobody is perfect. If your parents and teachers have taught you something, they have done it to the best of their knowledge. However, as a grown up, you might realise that you need to unlearn what you have learn and move ahead in life. Of course, we assume that you will use this discretion with honesty and unlearn only what was affecting your mental enrichments. Trying to unlearn that $2 \times 2 = 4$ would be a silly step to take.

Some of us have been told we are good for nothing so many times that we have come to believe that about ourselves. Being told that one is not good looking, or that one is stupid, or even that one is not good at what they are passionate about — if we are told such things too many times, we start believing them. But it is important to know your own self-worth and in needed, unlearn to learn new things.

Now that you have started your journey of self-discovery with me, I must make it clear that it involves unlearning old principles to learn new principles. Here is an activity to set the ball rolling.

I am providing you a list of some firm principles which you have learnt in your formative years. Tick the option as per your wish only:

1. I have to work so hard for living. ....
2. I can't afford more to buy my house. ....

3. I don't feel good as I am from a poor family. ....
4. My family is responsible for my unsuccessful career. ....
5. I am made to strive for what I want........................
6. People don't understand my feelings so I like to be alone. ....
7. I don't deserve the best as I am not a great person like others. ....
8. I should not multitask; I should do one task at a time ....
9. I can't be the person like other great people because they have been more fortunate. ....
10. I have my limitations so I can't stretch beyond a point ....

After conducting several sessions with my student groups, I have found that most people think that the above sentences are right. These firm beliefs have contributed in a large measure to the course their lives have taken. They used to live hard lives because they had only one option to work hard, to blame others, to complain about everything, etc.

Sometimes you become a slave of fixed ideas which you have been following for many years. It is like a habit. You don't know whether it is right or wrong. You take it for granted and never try to test or determine its value even if it is a worthless idea. You need to unlearn such useless ideas to learn new and valuable ones.

When you think that you have to go through a lot of books to pass the exams, trust me your exams become a daunting task because you have already decided to work hard for the study. Suppose you wish to buy your dream home but you don't think of purchasing as you lack the courage to do so. Actually, money is only a secondary issue but because you are fixated on the monetary aspect you do not even consider other feasible options before you. Imagine you are from a poor family background. You think thrice before purchasing anything because you

are always short on cash. You will never try to think of those luxuries which people enjoy. Why?? Not because you are poor! It's because you have put all luxuries out of your reach. Your environment and principles have made you a miser but you don't know that energy works in your body. You can change the frequency of your thoughts to receive positive energy because everything is energy. *Money Is Also Energy*. When you make a positive affirmation like '*I can do it, as it seems to be easy*' then your subconscious mind begins to respond to your positive vibrations.
Let's read some positive affirmations like-

1. I can do this.
2. I am able to pay my bills.
3. I receive money from everywhere.
4. It is easy for me to take decisions.
5. I am leading a great life.
6. I attract positive persons around me.
7. I love to enjoy my life.
8. I am above all problems.
9. God is always with me.
10. I deserve the best things in my life.

My beloved friends, I know very well that you think that your problems are bigger so how can these positive affirmations help you? Actually, whatever you think is just your opinion. Either you can or you cannot. Once you are convinced that you can do it, your subconscious mind throws back at you plenty of creative ideas. You start receiving wonderful thoughts to solve your present problems. You only need to act upon these ideas. *No* or *Yes* — both are your choices. If you say no to something, your mind gets ready to reply with NO IDEAS. If you say yes to something, your mind prepares to get back to you with YES IDEAS. This is a very common but great power which you all are provided with by the universe. Try to avoid doubts because they only serve to strengthen your negative responses. DON'T DOUBT, JUST FLOOD YOURSELF WITH POSITIVE AFFIRMATIONS.

****

REAL PEOPLE, REAL STORIES

Hey all, I am thrilled to share my experiences after being guided through this wonderful workshop. I worked on the Law of Attraction and the Vision Board. I was amazed to see that even during my non-working days, I was able to earn an amount, almost 100K, which many dream of. I was able to relax more, meditate and started practicing more of Reiki. The gift of Auto Writing also came along. It was easy for me to deal with my sinus issues, too. My son was having issues in his job and it all got settled. The success is all due to change in perception which was possible through the guidance of mentors. Warm wishes to Vikas, Rosie, Karen, ARTep and all my group members for motivating me with their inspirational stories. Vikas is a wonderful human being who must have been along with me for many life times. I love to remain in his guidance throughout the life.

Love You Universe!

Gurjeet Kour
Delhi, India

Hello! The workshop which has been started by Vikas has brought drastic change in my life — not only financially, but emotionally too. Within few weeks my whole negativity has been washed out and within a month I have started my own online business. Not only this, earlier I used to fall ill very often and I was thinking that my body does not have stamina to work. But now I am perfectly fit and fine. Today I am independent and confident. The money flows to me easily. I am like a shining star. I loved the session The law of you, Switch words and Attracting health & wealth.

Thank you so much Vikasji and all the mentors of the group.

Lots of Gratitude to you all!

Tanisha
Jaipur, Rajasthan

CHAPTER FOUR

How to motivate yourself?

"Infuse your life with action. Don't wait for it to happen. Make it happen. Make your own future. Make your own hope. Make your own love. And whatever your beliefs, honor your creator, not by passively waiting for grace to come down from upon high, but by doing what you can to make grace happen... yourself, right now, right down here on Earth."

~ Bradley Whitford ~

We all need a push ourselves once in a while. Sometimes, it is to take the plunge into the unknown and start something new, while sometimes it is simply to get up and go to office. Every time we have been in situations where we feel low and unsure of ourselves, or at the task at hand, someone comes along and pushes us to try harder. When we were kids and were afraid of exams, our parents and teachers encouraged us, "Come on, study a little more, you can do it!" As teenagers, when we felt like quitting, our friends encouraged us on,

"You're really good, you just need to focus, come on you can do it." When we got older, our colleagues and bosses urged us to excel, "You're so close to receiving that bonus, don't give up now, come on, you can do it!"

All these people in our lives have been 'motivating' us. They were boosting our spirits when our spirits were low and pushing us to excel. In simple words, motivation is *a push that makes you progress towards achieving your goal*.

But what if these people aren't around? What if you find yourself in a tough spot and, feel dejected and ready to quit, and no one comes along to push you?

That's when YOU need to MOTIVATE YOURSELF.

Self-motivation is a very important life skill that every individual needs to instil and develop. Why?

Because motivation is the driving force to achieving goals, and only by putting yourself in the driver's seat can you be certain to achieve every single mission you embark on. It is that simple. By taking control of what pushes you to accomplish your goals, you automatically ensure you are going to succeed.

John was 14 when he decided to learn to play the saxophone. His dream was completely different from all students in his music class, who went for more common instruments like the guitar, drums and the keyboard. He ran up to his mom, who was his strongest motivator and asked her, "Is it a good instrument to play, mom?" For the first time his mom was stumped, because she really didn't know.

He went to his dad who was also clueless and so were his friends. He then sat in his room, confused and dazed. He thought maybe it is a bad idea. Maybe he should just learn what everyone else is learning. Dejected, he put on his favourite 'Kenny G' record and waited for the saxophone solo to come up. John closed his eyes and imagined himself playing that solo for his family and friends. He could picture all of them smiling and clapping. He opened his eyes and told himself, "I want them to feel that way when I play. I want to be the best. I love the sound of the saxophone." John never looked back.

Think about it for a second. You have always had self-motivation, but you just didn't know it, or you probably called it by another by another name like guts, burning desires, passion, fire etc. When you decided to pick a major subject in college, or change your job, or go on a solo trip to an unknown location, or run a marathon, you might've gone to a hundred people for tips and encouragement but in the end, you sat and reflected the decision on your own. You wondered, "Is this a smart move? Can I really do this? What if I fail? What will I do next?" What happened then? You heard answers from within. Your mind, conscience and gut told you to take the step, the rest will be taken care of. Didn't that feel wonderful? When your mind was on your side, telling you, 'You can do it!' That is self-motivation!

Self-motivation not only drives you to succeed, it also makes you a confident person. You slowly learn not to rely on anyone for affirmation, you affirm your decisions yourself. This gives you immense courage to face challenges.

OK, so you have understood the importance of self-motivation but are still wondering, *How to build self-motivation? Is there a series of steps that can help you develop it?*

While self-motivation is very personal and should come from within, yes there is a routine that I follow, that has helped me personally. The next time you are in doubt, or confused about a decision try this:

— Sit in a silent place and calm your mind. Try to rid your mind of all thoughts and think of nothing.

Now think about the decision you have to make, or the goal you have to achieve. It could be:

- I want to run the 100m race.
- I want to change my job.
- I want to propose for marriage.
- I want to learn French. Whatever it is, just focus on it. Now ask yourself why you want to do it:
- I want to win the gold medal, it has always been my dream.
- My work is not interesting and I want a higher pay.

- I want to start a family.
- I want to visit France and experience the culture.

Now clear your mind completely and imagine you have achieved your goal

Picture standing on the podium holding the gold medal high for everyone to see.

Picture yourself in a new office rolling up your sleeves up, enjoying work and drawing a big pay check.

Imagine yourself in a park with your spouse and kids.

Imagine yourself under the Eiffel tower speaking to the locals in French.

Now open your eyes. The end result that you envisioned, how did that make you feel? Invincible?

Extremely happy? Like a superstar? Let that feeling drive you. Tell yourself, you will feel exactly that way, even better, when you achieve your goal. You will automatically get up and take the step towards your goal.

Take charge of your driving force and you will achieve everything and anything you pursue.

A few common ways to keep a positive attitude is by keeping a positive company. More often than not, the company we keep controls the attitude we have. If people around us are unambitious, their lack of positivity seeps through to us. Instead, if you surround yourself with people who are confident, bright and ambitious, the conversations surrounding you would also be on the same lines.

Your own personality is a work in progress. Do not get complacent and remain the way you are - always keep working on yourself and making yourself better. Evaluate yourself; work on yourself. With confidence and positive attitude will come the personality which will take you head in life.

You don't need to be the fastest, wisest, smartest and the most brilliant. All that you need is courage, boldness, the will to try and the faith to believe it is possible. All you need is to have faith in yourself, that you can do it. It is time to harness the lion in you.

Now I add one more word to motivation — *positive attitude*. A positive attitude and motivation can take you to the destination without fail. The positive attitude makes you stronger and motivation makes you act faster than you would normally. Both combined can make you a superman or a champion. You should balance both of these attributes in your life to lead a magical life.

It is motivation which helps you think positively and enthuses you to do something great whereas positive attitude helps you to work assiduously till you attain your goal.

"It always seems impossible until it's done"

~ Nelson Mandela ~

REAL PEOPLE, REAL STORIES

Hello!! I am a very happy soul and beloved to all. I had always wished to have a great family and by the grace of God, I am blessed with the beautiful family. I always find beauty in others to make myself beautiful. I take my physical body as the universe's gift so I adore it as a temple. I do Yoga and meditation everyday and I keep myself away from all negativities. Since I met with Vikas and came across with his teachings which are introduced in this book "The Hidden Spark". My life has become more juice up and spiritually inclined because I had a wish to have a son who could understand my inner and pure soul affection and motherly attachment that I found in Vikas. I am deeply blessed to have him. I liked the sessions of this book because it is based on practical issues-solving and I got a great supports from the mentors too.

With best regards

Shefali Trivedi
Indore, MP

Hello from Ivory Coast!!

Dreams really do come true when we follow the law of attraction, switch words, thinking positive and so many more things..Incredible right? Yes, all the credit goes to "The Magical Workshop" conducted by Mr Vikas. In the beginning of this work shop (session no 1st & 2nd), we were asked to write what we actually want and I made a collage of things which I really wanted and started following the instructions of our mentors. One of my dream was "HONOUR ROLL" for my son, that was missing since 1 year. I badly wanted it back. And YES YES YES my son got honour roll with very good percentage. I am beyond grateful for Mr Vikas, Rosie ma'am, Ms Hiral and Karen ma'am their precious time, knowledge and patience. I am so happy to tell that some of my dreams are in process and will definitely come true with flying colours.

Thank you so much!

Mrs. Anita Aacharya
Ivory coast, South Africa

CHAPTER FIVE

REMOVE YOUR MENTAL BLOCKAGES

You cannot have a positive life and a negative mind

~ Joyce Meyer ~

Before you understand how to remove mental blockages, you must understand your mind. They say it is all in our minds. The state of your mind decides whether you'll be poor or rich, strong or weak, fast or slow, happy or sad.

Once a scientist thought of doing research on a person who was about to die. So he went to jail and found a murderer who had already been sentenced to death by hanging. Fortunately, he got the permission from the judge to experiment on the criminal. He took the culprit to an open space and made him sit on a chair and tied his hands and legs with a rope. The scientist warned him that he would release the rattle snake (which he was then holding in his hand) on his body if he did not come with the truth regarding the crime allegedly committed by him.

The paranoid criminal literally squeaked that he was telling the truth and requested for mercy. One man covered his face and the scientist came closer to him to whisper into his ears that he would now be bitten by the poisonous snake. Suddenly, the scientist pricked him hard with a safety pin on his leg and he died instantly as if the rattle snake had bit him.

The bottom line: Mind is all powerful. The criminal was not bitten by the snake but the fear of the snake killed him even though he was pricked by a small safety pin.

The human mind is composed of two parts: Conscious and Subconscious. Your *conscious mind* helps you focus properly. It lends you the ability to distinguish between the real and the unreal. If you constantly focus on your negative thoughts then the sub conscious will deliver feelings, emotions and memories that are associated with that type of thinking.

When you focus on positive thoughts you will feel a lot more comfortable. The ability of your conscious mind to direct your attention and awareness is one of the most important powers you have. To make some changes in your life, you must learn to control what you consciously focus on. Make a choice and stick to it. This creates your destiny. When you place your attention on something it can be easily distracted. Focus is a finer level of attention. Focus on your attention. Think of a spotlight and direct your attention like a laser beam.

You can control what you focus on. It involves your mind, what you look at and what you think about. When you become more focused on one thing you become less aware of what else is going on around you. The more aware you become of your surroundings the less you focus. In social situations focus on others, appreciate others, look for positive aspects of others and the conscious mind will reflect these back on you. If you want to control your emotions better or gain better results, then shift your focus. It will help you to think, feel and behave in a totally different way.

What does your subconscious mind do?
It communicates via emotions, feelings, sensations and reflexes, images and dreams. It doesn't communicate in words. It obeys orders. Your conscious mind is in charge whereas the sub conscious mind will deliver emotions and feelings of what you continually think about.

By consciously being in charge of your own thoughts through directing your focus and using visualisation, you can influence what programs the subconscious mind constantly runs. I would like to share how changing your habits will change your life. What are habits and why do they matter? Your habits are key to who you are and the change you want. Lasting change, i.e. achieving your goals, is not the result of a one-off transformation but a product of daily habits. What do you want to achieve? What do you want to change? Whatever it is, getting it is the result of your habits.

Habits play a role in what you look and feel like, in your success and relationships. So, what are habits? Habits are the things we do, but also and maybe as importantly, the way we think and what we believe. They include the self-beliefs that influence what we do, our behaviour and the actions we take. A habit is the repeated thinking and behaviours that become automatic, so we don't mostly think about them. Many of our everyday activities involve habits with a cue, action and reward. Here's a few you probably repeatedly do and don't really think about them: cleaning your teeth, tying your laces or riding a bike.

Learning to drive is painfully slow as you have to think of each step every time. Once it becomes an ingrained habit driving is a simple, uncomplicated exercise. Sometimes you can't even remember driving somewhere. Then there are certain behavioural patterns we get into which quickly become habits like going to bed or getting up early or late and eating certain types of food or at certain times of the day. There also are habits which you think of as bad or unhelpful. Biting your nails, picking your nose, procrastination, being distracted by social media and emails, and eating snacks late at night. We need to know how we form habits in order to change them. Habits have certain characteristics. Cues, routines and rewards. There's a cue that initiates the behaviour. A cue is a trigger, or reminder, something that triggers our thought or behaviour. Like the cue line in a play, (the line before you come in) which on hearing it reminds you to say your line, or triggers you to deliver your line. Cue is followed by the routine. This is the behaviour or action that the cue has triggered and the bit we think of as the habit.

This is followed by the third part of a habit — the reward. This is the bit that is of benefit to you in some way, even though it might not actually feel like that. As it's a reward or benefit your brain wants you to repeat it. Once you've done it often enough it becomes a habit.

Why habits matter?

Habits matter because they hold great influence and sway over how we think, act and feel which just about covers everything we do. We get into habits of thinking, doing and feeling. This, then becomes automatic behaviour. *We become what we repeatedly do, think or feel.* This is great if it's a good automatic behaviour but what if it's not good behaviour? Bad habits, don't support us in the changes we want to make and the way we want to live.

That's why habits matter. They matter to us because they are such a big part of who we are and what we want to do. The results of their influence are felt and seen in every aspect of our life and work. They help to determine how we feel and what we do.

Habits underpin our mind management. Habits matter because lasting change is a product of daily habits. The little things we do day in day out, week in week out and then month in month out, go into making the person we are, how we think, feel and act. In other words, we and our lives are the sum and result of our habits.

Let us take an example many people can identify with. There was this boy Saurabh, who had reached that stage in life where he realised how importance it was to have a healthy lifestyle. To sleep on time, wake up early, eat right, exercise a bit, socialise and stay away from too much of gadgets. His mind was made and he made resolution to implement from the next day. But the next day never came. Not because Saurabh was not serious about his vow, or he was taking it lightly. He was trying, no doubt. But the habits he had formed over years, needed time to change. He was used to sleeping late, waking up late, not eating home food, eating at office canteen, drinking every night with friends and not exercising at all. Ten years of such habits could not be broken overnight. And this began his struggle. Now to break these habits, he needs to train his mind and that is the only way, he can change his habits. Only time will change if Saurabh will be able to change his lifestyle. While everybody else will see the outcome of a changed lifestyle, only Saurabh will know that it was by training his mind, that he could achieve this.

What is mind work? What can we do about it? Before we think about how to change our habits — we need to identify them and decide which are helpful and which are not serving us in what we want to do or the person we want to be. Mind work is to take a whole day to really notice what you think are your habits. Notice what you do and how you feel, and note down a word or two, otherwise you'll forget. You think you won't, but you really will, and then, see if it's linked to a habit and if that habit is helping or hindering you.

To take it one step further, you can relate it to the three aspects of a habit. This will not only help you determine if it actually is a habit but also help you understand what triggers it (the cue) how it shows itself (the routine or behaviour or action) and what that habit is doing for you (this is the reward and benefits bit). This will not only give you an increased level of self-awareness and understanding but will enable you to change the habits that are not serving you.

"Don't let mental blocks control you, set yourself free. Comfort your fear and turn the mental blocks into building blocks,"

~ Roopleen ~

****

REAL PEOPLE, REAL STORIES

Hello friends! I am a Rekie Healer, Spiritual Healer, Mantra Sadhna, Water Healing, and Law of Attraction Practitioner. I am a highly spiritual person but the moment I joined the workshop, I had got strong positive vibrations. The mentors from different countries not only guided me about spirituality but also provided me the about the enlightenment and the ultimate goal of my life. The sessions "The law of karma, the of you, the law of attraction and meditation" portions assisted me a lot. I would like to say that this book can be a very handy to ambitious. I released my all negative energies and restarted my life after being refreshed by this workshop.

Thank you so much all!

Bhawana Trivedi
Indore, India

Hello guys!! I have changed a lot after applying the ways the mentors have advised to us in workshop especially dealing with serious mental, financial and family issues. The way I see myself, money, dreams, success, relationship, everything has changed for me now. I was suffering from having no self-love and self-respect before joining this session. Now I see myself in a new version, the best version of myself. My life has started changing. I started loving my job and I made triple income in last summer. I must say that it's a huge improvement and change during my teaching life. It's my great fortune to be a member of the workshop. Thank u so much all of my mentors from deep of my heart and specially my bro Vikas. I was always in need of brother in my life which has been taken by Vikas bhaiya in my life.

Gayatri Karke
Myanmar

CHAPTER SIX

THE MAGICAL LAW OF ATTRACTION

"The law of attraction is the answer to all that has been, all that is and all that will ever be",

~ Ralph Waldo Emerson ~

You are all human beings, which mean you all have a mind. Having a mind means having the ability to think and that means *The Law Of Attraction*. Yes! To think about something for a long time allows the law of attraction to work. This law is pretty popular among the new generation. While the younger generation knows about this law, I have my doubts about how aware they are of it. The law of attraction is very useful and beneficial when you come to know the exact method to use it to manifest your dreams. In this chapter, I will explain this great law in detail.

Actually, *The Law of Attraction* is the reflection of you. If you are rich today, credit goes to the law of attraction, if you are sad about something (e.g) about any mishaps, the responsibility of that lies on the law of attraction too. There is a great power which works behind the law of attraction and makes you feel that this law exists in the universe. When you want to attain something or maybe you have some desire or perhaps you want to do something, you automatically start thinking about that particular thing/activity. When you think about something, it means that you are in that frequency where you can visualize it. Once you visualize it, you have got the power to hold it in your brain. Your brain sends out those waves out of your mind to the nature and the nature in turn, conveys your message to the universe while the universe makes arrangements in a way that you want things to manifest.

Let me narrate a real life tale which was told by one of the attendee during my workshop. The boy who told the story was in love with a girl who too loved him a lot. They were in a relationship for about eight years. They made many promises to each other for their future. They were both studying at that point and both you were unaware of what their families' verdicts would be. It turned out that neither of their families wanted that relationship at all. The girl's father wanted his daughter to be a doctor and sent her to another city. The boy too was to be sent to another city for his further studies. Before separating, the boy decided to take his love to their families to confess their relationship to them. When the girl was asked by the boy for the marriage in front of their families, the girl kept mum for some time and finally she refused to marry him. Instead she said, she wanted to focus on her dream to become a doctor. The boy was humiliated by both families at that time. He was shocked to hear the love of his life said such a thing. They both separated for many years, but the boy kept holding a grudge in his heart. He tried to forget her, but failed. Instead, he started hating her. He started to scream whenever he remembered the memories they had together. 5 years went by and one day that boy received a message from her, asking him to marry her. He was shell-shocked, but he refused her proposal.

After telling me the story till here, the boy asked me, "If she didn't want to be in his life till then, why did she want to come back to him?

I asked him if he loved her or hated her. He said, "I hate her a lot."

To this I asked him, "Do you try to forget her every day. He said, "Yes! I want to erase her from my life."

Hearing his reply, I told him, "You attracted her back in your life simply by hating her and thinking about her." When you focus on something for a long period of time, the law of attraction always works. It does not matter if you are doing it intentionally or unintentionally, you are a kid or old, you are a male or a female, you are an Indian or a foreigner, you are poor or rich. According to me, "The more you try to remember, the more you forget. The more you try to forget, the more you remember." So, simply try to divert your mind by getting yourself busy in doing the tasks you love to do, if you don't feel comfortable with the tasks, better be with your friends or go for a vacation.

What is the Law of Attraction?

Each and every human in the world is provided by three most wonderful powers:

- The thoughts you hold in your mind.
- The positive vibrations you feel.
- The actions you take towards your goal.

Once you become aware of these three powerful things, you can be a master of your life. You might have read many inspirational books and found the common message in them all telling that you must be positive towards your goal or never give up your dreams or have faith in yourself or you are the destiny maker. What exactly is the meaning of that?

The meaning of this is to let you know about the three most wonderful powers which you are not aware of the thoughts you think, the vibrations you feel and the actions you take. When you become aware of these powers, the law of attraction begins to work for you.

A key part of the *Law of Attraction* explains that where you place your focus can have an intense impact on what happens to you. If you spend your days wallowing in regrets about the past or fears of the future, you'll likely see more negativity appearing, but if you look for the silver lining in every experience, then you'll soon start to see positivity surrounding you every day. Therefore, the *Law of Attraction* encourages you to see that you have the freedom to take control of how your future develops, shaping it in the ways you choose.

When you learn how to use the many powerful and practical tools associated with the *Law of Attraction*, you can start living and thinking in a more optimistic manner that is specifically designed to attract even more positive events and experiences. Whatever you're longing for, whatever your dreams and goals are, the *Law of Attraction* can teach valuable lessons that will bring you closer to your most treasured ambitions.

How can you use the Law of Attraction in your life?

Although there is a lot of worth to even simply learning what the Law of Attraction is, you can really start using it to its full potential when you begin to understand that it can be used in subtle ways every minute of the day. Becoming more mindful of your own thoughts helps you discover what you should keep or remove from your own mind and the reality your experience. Once you are aware of this, you will yourself pay more attention to the negativity within and fight it with your own fresh beliefs and positive mindsets. With this, what happens is that you start seeing what you truly want from your future and you can then go on to list down your clearer goals with actionable steps at every stage.

There are many different ways of putting to use, your knowledge of the *Law of Attraction* into your everyday life. Just let the new things you have learnt, flourish all through the day. Just hearing this much might sound like a tedious task to take up, but the truth remains that simple changes have powerful consequences when you're working with the *Law of Attraction*. After a few weeks of practicing your new approach, most of the things would come to you naturally and become second nature.

Affirmations and the Law of Attraction:-

Law of Attraction Affirmations can take the form of internal thoughts or spoken words, but they can also be represented visually. Irrespective of how you choose to use them, you can design them to reflect your vision of how you want your life to change. For example, many people stand in front of the mirror and say out loud, some positive words which induce the feeling of success. By using many positive affirmations and desirable lines, you can change the frequency of your thoughts and the way you see the things like "I am very powerful and healthy." This statement itself gives you physical and mental strengths. Once you speak the positive thoughts to yourself that sends the positive vibes to your mind and your mind sends out the positive vibes to the nature. The nature brings you towards more positive people and you allow the law of attraction to work for you.

This book is offering you some affirmations below:-

1. I HAVE A WONDERFUL, HAPPY AND A FULFILLING LIFE.
2. I RECEIVE ALL THE ABUNDANCE THE UNIVERSE HAS TO OFFER.
3. I AM SUCCESSFUL IN ALL I CHOOSE TO DO.
4. I AM BECOMING RICHER EVERYDAY.
5. I AM SO DEEPLY GRATEFUL FOR EVERY CELL IN MY BODY.
6. I FIND NEW THINGS TO FEEL GRATEFUL FOR EVERYDAY. MY LIFE IS FILLED WITH ABUNDANCE.
7. MY HEART IS OPEN; I SPEAK WITH LOVING WORDS.
8. I FEEL JOY AND CONTENTMENT IN THIS MOMENT RIGHT NOW.
9. EVERY DAY AND IN EVERY WAY, I AM GETTING BETTER AND BETTER.
10. ABUNDANCE FLOWS FREELY THROUGH ME.
11. I EXCEL IN ALL THAT I DO, AND SUCCESS COMES EASILY TO ME.
12. I CAN AND WILL HAVE MORE THAN I EVER DREAMED POSSIBLE.
13. I ALWAYS HAVE ENOUGH MONEY FOR MYSELF.
14. I AM SO GRATEFUL FOR EVERY PERSON AND EVERY THING IN MY LIFE.
15. EVERY DAY I GIVE THANKS FOR MY WONDERFUL LIFE.

How do you think good thoughts?
The answer is to pay attention to your **feelings**. Your thoughts lead to feelings. Your feelings tell you whether you are on the right track or not.

If you feel good, you are thinking good thoughts.

~ Rhonda Byrne ~

If you feel bad, you need to stop feeling bad or else, by the *Law of Attraction*, you will attract bad things in your life. So, how do you stop feeling bad? This is a complicated question, and the answer is going to depend on the person and the situation. But find a way, do something, correct something to stop feeling bad!

Why? Because thoughts and feelings, which are caused by your thoughts have a frequency. If you feel bad, you are emitting a negative frequency and unfortunately that negative frequency will be reflected in your life. If you feel good, that positive frequency will attract positive things to your life.

What are good feelings?
The vibrations which make you a happy soul, is called good feelings like love, happiness, comfort, satisfaction, mental peace, gratitude, joy, delights, hopes, positivity etc, .

Bad vibrations which disturb or distract you or make you feel bad, are called bag feelings like anger, frustrations, bad emotions, unhappiness, downhearted attitude, arrogance, ego etc

If you want to use the law of attraction to manifest your dreams and aims, you must be aware of your vibrations because your vibrations decide what kind of feelings you are having and your feelings send out the frequency out to the environment which attracts the same feelings further towards you.

That's why it is suggested that you should feel happy because as you feel happy you send out the positive vibes in the universe and help you more to attract the same feelings. If you want to succeed in your life then think about the success, the more you think about the success, the more positive vibrations you send out to the universe and helps you more to manifest it as fast as you send out the positive vibes. If you want to have more wealth and fine health, you need to think about them. Your energy flows where your thought goes, so be careful of thinking about the thing you wish to have in your life. Think about the money, think about the big house you want to live in, see yourself as a very healthy person whatever you are running on your mind the same you are going to hold in your life. Of course, hard work is also a pre-requisite, but no amount of hard work will take you closer to your goals if the general attitude in your mind is negative.

There is a modern science called Quantum Physics that supports the existence of the *Law of Attraction*. Quantum physics teaches that everything is energy, because if you break anything down to its simplest form, it is an atom, and if you break an atom, you have — energy. Since everything is energy, and a thought is a thing, with a frequency, you will, thoughts affect our universe. Quantum physics says that our world is shaped by our thoughts.

> *"Quantum physics says that you can't have a universe without mind entering into it, and that the mind is actually shaping the very thing that is being perceived."*
>
> ~ Dr. Fred Alan Wolf ~

Positive language helps you manifest what you want. This is very fact that whatever you speak, you will attract the same in you life because by speaking the words you command the universe about your wishes. The words work faster than feels because your words decide what you feel. Conscious creation should be easy, if you're working at all - you're working too hard.

If I talk about the manifestation, to manifest something is like to get ready to receive the results from the universe which can be virtually because you need to have faith for the wishes you have. In which you need to pretend to receive that thing already or you need to pretend to be the person you want to be. Stop thinking about the questions like How, When, Where these all will happen? You just need to feel it coming to you. Sometimes you go wrong by over thinking because once you think about something that's great but as you think more about it that brings doubts too towards you so better think about your goal, set a plan, act upon it and manifest it. Think yourself being at that place you want to be. Think yourself receiving all things that you want. This process does not cost anything whereas it activates your mental broadness and allows the law of attraction to work faster for you.

Only you can save yourself, the same only you can achieve your goals so do not stop yourself from thinking high because if you are aiming high, it means you have a great potentials to have it in your life. The universe has sent you here to achieve something very big and great which seems impossible to others.

"Focus only on what you want"

~ The Secret ~

****

REAL PEOPLE, REAL STORIES

I was not comfortable in sharing my tragedy with you at all because it might upset you but later on I decided to do that because I really don't want to see others suffering from HIV, AIDS. I confess that I was going to commit suicide because I had no hope to live longer. I had been widowed thrice because I married three times. I had four children from my all three husbands. My first husband had died from cancer, second died in an accident and the third left me alone. I was shaken by the news that I am an HIV positive. My family kicked me out with my four kids. I had no shelter and money to buy milk in order to feed my kids. I somehow managed to find a shelter. I finally decided to die but it was a coincidence that I saw Vikas's post on a social media site one night and it said, "If you have wasted 99% of your life, then still think about 1% life that is in your hand". I messaged him and said, "I am going to die so please pray for me to bless a good life next time". He said, "That's fine but God won't bless you a good life because you are going to end the most beautiful life which is already given it to you." His words touched my heart and I started crying. I cried for his help, although he is much younger to me but in knowledge, he is an expert. He gave me two days to think about choosing two options in my life "Do or Die". I instantly messaged him that I want to do but he replied me after two days that, "That's great". He was ready to help me. I asked him about getting rid of my fatal disease HIV. He simply said that it is curable if you want, just remove the tag from your mind that I am an HIV patient. He advised me to focus on being physically strong. Later on I joined his workshop and I improved myself a lot. At present I am healthy and wealthy. My one son is studying in Kenya and one daughter has her own business. My other two children help me in my personal business which is highly grown now. I support other HIV patients to live the life happily because the real medicine is within you. Today, the society respects me because I did not give up and did something great as human being. Vikas is a legendary man. He is a brainy man who thinks everything practically. I bless him everyday. Today I run for 5 km without issues. I am totally fine now. The best session for me was "Age is just a number". All mentors are wonderful souls and Vikas, hats off to you, man!! Bless you!!

Alvaa Dock
Nigeria
ς

CHAPTER SEVEN

THE LAW OF YOU

"what worries you, masters you"

~ John Locke ~

What do you see when you look into a mirror? The mirror reflects your exact copy. Ever heard the story of the hungry dog? He went to and fro in search of food and finally got a piece of bread. While crossing a bridge, he saw another dog holding a piece of bread in his mouth. He coveted that piece too so he growled and stared menacingly at the other dog. Every action produced an identical counter reaction. At last he opened his mouth to bark. His bread fell down and the dog disappeared from the scene.

Was there any another dog in the water? No!! The dog's reflection was there to copy him. "The Reflection" is not the reflection. The Law of Duality in metaphysics propounds that there are two copies of everything in the universe. That is why it is said that "What you give you receive".

Just think about your present woes (any kind of major or minor problems) which hold you back and write down below and seek solutions by yourself without taking anyone's help. By the time you finish this chapter you will be able to solve your problems:

1. _____
2. _____
3. _____

4. _____
5. _____

Have you ever considered the though process in the mind of a criminal before he has actually committed a crime? He flits between a yes and no repeatedly till he is able to justify that action. Imagine a situation where you covet your friend's wrist watch and finally decide to steal it. You know that it is a sin but sometimes your mind leads you astray. As you try to steal that watch your inner soul stops you from doing it, but on the other hand, you get tempted to steal it. Again the soul stops but your body moves toward it. This moment is called The Law of You.

The Law of You is responsible for this chaos. The Law of You is just a mental state. When your inner soul becomes more attentive than your body, the Law of You begins.

Many people come to me with different problems seeking solutions in my workshops. Some of them are repentant while some have even contemplated suicide in desperate circumstances. To guide them I take help from The Law of You. I always tell all my friends to listen to their inner soul because that's You and one can never do wrong to oneself. I would like to pull your attention towards spirituality and what our holy books have to say about The Law of You.

Some chapters in Bhagvad Gita are about "Body & Soul" & what is the differentiation between the two. Body is said to be perishable while the Soul is immortal. Lord Sri Krishna in Bhagvad Gita says, 'you should consider yourself as that immortal Soul'. Soul, Spirit, Atmaa, Self etc. are words which are used to define subtle nature of ourselves which is invisible & mysterious. Soul is something which is within this body & something which can exist without this body. The physical body reacts to object in this material world. Soul is indestructible & immortal. It moves from one body to the other. You are not able to see this Soul but The Law of You brings you closer to it.

The holy Bible also talks about the body and soul. It says one can reach the almighty through the soul. The soul is immortal whereas body

The Hidden Spark

is temporary form which has been given to you to do something great for humanity. No one is immortal in this world, you all have to die but the thing is, how you make use of this life. The sacred Quran also talks about the soul and body. God has given you body to connect your soul to the supreme power

Suppose your name is Vikas that's not a single Vikas, that's two. First is internal and second is external. Your soul can be your best friend and companion but you always ignore it's voice of that and succumb to the pressure created by your immediate circumstances.

You only need to listen to your inner voice which is the eternal truth. It leads you to the correct path and tells you what is right and wrong. The universe has provided you with the best Guide who lies within you and stays with you till your last breath. There is no problem in the world whose answers are not known to your inner soul. Just follow the voice and trust the universe because The Law of You exists and works always in your favour.

REAL PEOPLE, REAL STORIES

First of all, thank you very much for this awesome money workshop. You are doing a very great work of improving people's lives. Now coming to my success story, after joining the workshop there has been a lot of inner transformation in me. I became more confident more active and mainly more positive. My trust on Law of Attraction has also increased. In last 3-4 months I got job of salary Rs. 30,000. It is my first job after Graduation. The profile given is also related to my interest. Actually I tagged in other IT domain before but by gratitude and LOA again I got my desired profile. Thanks to you. My training on technology was also awesome. In between training, while background check there is one criminal case found on me (by mistake of same name). My job was almost gone and career was finished but again LOA helped me and on my birthday only I got clearance that it's not me. After training, the most crucial part came the location where I had to work. I wanted Pune. But I got Bangalore. No vacancies in Pune. Luckily someone wanted Bangalore so I changed with him to Mumbai. But again I was not happy. My destination was Pune. I worked in Mumbai for one month. Again one more miracle happened which was almost impossible for me. Vacancy created in Pune and there is no one from my technology in Pune. I requested them they

take my interview and here now I am in my Pune. I have many more plans to work here now lots of business plans. Right now I know my income is low but surely I will make it awesome with the help of you. My first target it to make it to Rs. 50000 by end of this year and I am working on it. In between, I also faced some difficulties like death of my father and my severe illness. But I successfully recovered from it now. Really you made a great transformation in me and made my life beautiful and I am feeling for last few months that my monthly income and health both have increased a lot. All credit goes to Vikas Trivedi's workshop and mentors for their time and knowledge they shared with us free of cost in this financial word.

                Tons of Gratitude!

                                Amol
                        Pune, Maharashtra

CHAPTER EIGHT

Reverse Psychology

I try to lie as much as I can when I'm interviewed. It's reverse psychology. I figure if you lie, they'll print the truth.

~ River Phoenix ~

Reverse Psychology is a technique that involves the special behaviour that is opposite to the one desired, with the expectation that you will encourage the subject or persuade one to do what actually *is* desired, the opposite of what is suggested. This is one of the best techniques to use to persuade someone as per your wish. According to Theory of Psychology, Reverse Psychology is quite different but here I am presenting the Reverse Psychology in easier way to get the hang of the perfect concept. I tell you a story to connect you with the Reverse Psychology. Once the police was informed that there was a bomb in the main market and the bomber was seen walking down to the street. The police officers team divided into two teams first headed to the main market with the bomb squad and the second went after the bomber to chase him. The bomb squad checked the bomb and found it not diffusible as it was a plastic bomb so was needed to remove a specific wire. Now they had one option to get the bomber who could tell them about the wire who had already gone so far but the second team was after him. After some time, the bomber was caught and enquired about the specific wire to be removed but he was not ready to tell. The police kept asking him and at last he said, "Red wire must be removed". The police officer called to the bomb squad to inform them about that wire but he slightly observed that the bomber was asking them to remove wire as soon as possible to diffuse the bomb. He kept on forcing the police man to have the red wire removed. He was pretty sure that the wire hadn't been removed yet but the police man was not speaking anything on the call as he doubted him. He asked the bomb squad that, "Is there any other wire?" They replied, yes, "There is a green wire here." On the other hand, the bomber was not letting them cut the green cord and kept asking them to remove red one cord. Finally, the police and the bomb squad decided to remove the green wire. And that is when the bomb got diffused after removing the green cord and the bomber was arrested. Now the question is, where was the Reverse Psychology used and to where'd it failed? The bomber was asking them to remove red cord instead of green cord. At the very first, the police counted on him but due to his excess insistence they became suspicious on him, which is why he couldn't outwit the police man. This story covers both portions, if you use it carefully, you can achieve everything and persuade anyone easily but you use it in an improper way then it will not provide you the best results.

Suppose two people are arguing over some issues, their argument leads them to fight and become enemies. If you keep one person away from this argument then what would happen? Would that argument go further or become foes to each other? The answer may be, "No!!"

Imagine your life is free from tensions, frustrations, physical issues, mental issues, financial issues etc. What do you think of your life then? How will it be? Of course, your life will be beautiful. You will take yourself the way you want only.

How to use the Reverse Psychology

Before I explain more about the Reverse Psychology, I have divided the concept in two parts —

> Pretend to be the opposite of your point of view (Manipulation).
> Reverse your mind to oppose your negativity (Ignorance).

Pretend to be the opposite of your point of view whenever someone forbids you to do something; your **sense of freedom is difficult**. Your natural reaction becomes to **protest/rebel**. Then you can manipulate someone successfully.

The Reverse Psychology is such a key important technique for making others does what you want. You achieve it by telling them NOT to do it!

Wilson and Lassiter conducted a Reactance Theory to illustrate how reverse psychology works in 1982.

They managed to **create a desire for drawing sheets that initially was found unattractive**.

Here they experimented:-

The experimenters saw kids playing with various drawing sheets, which allowed them to identify one colour that was left mostly unused – the unattractive colour. They divided the children in two groups – the first group was asked to draw with any of the colours they wanted. But the second group was asked to draw with all of the colours except that one colour – the one they initially didn't like. Later, both groups of kids were given a chance to draw with the colour.

What was observed is that in the second group, the kids played 3 times longer with the forbidden colour.

When the same experiments were held on adults that showed similar results - **when you refuse people to use a certain object, it becomes more desirable/achievable.**

So, if you want somebody to do something for you, tell them they can't do it and what will happen is that they will want it more and they will rebel against your restriction to reassert their freedom – eventually doing exactly what you wanted them to.

(Taken experiment resource from the site-psychologyformarketers.com)

> Boredom is just the reverse side of fascination: both depend on being outside rather than inside a situation, and one leads to the other.
>
> ~ Arthur Schopenhauer ~

Reverse your mind to oppose your negativity, this portion covers your mental stability or I can say the ability to ignore something/someone.

Reverse your mind from the current situations or avert your attention from the present circumstances that you do not like. This is human tendency that you feel bad when you pay attention towards any matter, if that matter is good then you will feel good, if that matter is bad then you will not feel good. It means that your energy works here because you flow your energy towards that matter. Better just divert your mind like if someone is trying to drag you in backbiting or argument; in that situation just make an excuse and go away from that place. If someone is scolding you, better be silent or move away. If something which holds you back or your past bad memories distract you from your goals, just try not to listen or pay attention towards it. Because whatever you are facing; it's just a temporary stroke which comes to your mind to distract you only. Try to ignore everything which ails you. You can also ignore your pain, people, animals, birds, noise, cries, tensions, frustrations etc.

The reverse psychology does work when you use it in a proper way. Just ignore all unwanted things, these all unwanted things will be disappeared automatically.

> Actions are right in proportion as they tend to promote happiness; wrong as they tend to produce the reverse of happiness. By happiness is intended pleasure and the absence of pain.
>
> ~ John Stuart Mill ~

****

REAL PEOPLE, REAL STORIES

Hello! It all started in the month of November when I was thinking about increasing my prospects of financial prosperity. As they say, the Universe matches our vibrations and brings us closer to the opportunities that make our dreams come true, I came across a post on Face book by a dynamic person about a Workshop on How to Attract Money into our lives. I still remember those eligibility criteria for the Workshop that would be held for nearly a period of six months at zero cost. What struck me the most was that those who missed the instructions and did a mistake while asking for the enrolment for the workshop were pointed their indiscipline in reading the instructions. And I thought, this is one serious and committed coach and knows what to do, unlike many people who claim to do the best but end up below the expectations. The next indication towards my Journey of Financial Prosperity came when I was one of the lucky people who were shortlisted for the workshop. I'd quit my job for a change of career, and my bank balance was around Rs.50000 which was my savings. My next step in my career was an admission to doctoral research programme and hence, any kind of income was out of question. To fend for myself, I'd to attract money through various sources. The Workshop came to me as the *Right Opportunity* at the *Right Time*. We were introduced to a host of well trained and expert coaches, who are always on the go to help us clear our doubts and enable us to open our minds to Financial Prosperity. The results started manifesting to me in the form of an opportunity to interact with a Financial Planner and guidance to Financial Planning that I'd been waiting for many years. This happened in the last week of February, exactly around 45 days after the Money Workshop started. In fact, I'd no money to pay the Financial Planner and the teachings of the Workshop helped me attract the required money to pay the Financial Planner. Then came March, April, May and it's June now as I'm writing my story, and my bank balance stands at 1.5 lakh rupees. This sum might look small but this is a sum apart from all my commitments. To add to this, my Fellowship application for PhD has been processed and very soon I'll start receiving my Fellowship allowance too. Additionally, I've been able to mobilize some more money to make investments for higher returns. While all these sound fictional, I vouch that it is belief that dreams definitely come true that manifest everything. In a span of six months, my mindset has been changed to prosperity mindset. My mental blocks are replaced with open mindedness and a perception of possibilities. Gratitude has become my Lifestyle. While I speak of Gratitude, I would do Injustice if I don't thank my coaches Ms. Karen, Ms. Rosie and others in the

Money Workshop. Lastly, but the most importantly, I've to mention that this Workshop came a reality from just an idea because of that one person who posted on Social sites about this Amazing Opportunity, and the Workshop's Success is Meaningless without mentioning Mr. Vikas Trivedi (fondly called as Vikku). I fall short of words to describe his generosity, his willingness to help people and his determination to push people towards their dreams. He's given us hopes; hopes that our Dreams Come True. In fact, most of them have come true while the Workshop is still not over. I extend my infinite Gratitude to Vikku. I'm grateful to the Universe for blessing us with a coach like Vikku who has been selflessly making difference in many lives. Vikku, my best wishes to you always. May the Universe shower Abundance on you in all walks of life.

Nishita Swaminathan
Mysore, India

CHAPTER NINE

God's Call (A silent Ring)

When you hear the term God's Call, you might think that there will be a call from God or an important thought or a successful plan or a wonderful victory.

Let me first ask you a question, "What is your aim in your life?"

Suppose you don't have any aim in your life yet, then how will you find your aim?

Well, you have approximately 70,000 thoughts per day of which 40% thoughts come in your mind randomly, 30% wander into your mind aimlessly, 20% are useful, 5% thoughts you have in your mind are wishes or day dreams and the rest of 5% you have; are called very important thoughts which are also known to be called the signals from the subconscious mind but here I present as God's call.

I am going to talk about some famous people who had failed before they succeeded but they didn't give up in their goals and listened to their God's call. They pushed themselves hard to become the people they were destined to be and their names have become synonymous with success in their respective fields of study, technology, sports, social work etc.

The main question is, how did they succeed? By working hard, by the right direction or guidance, by using the law of attraction, or by the grace of God?

The exact answer is that they paid attention and listened to their God's call. Without having the important thought, without listening to the silent ring from God, you can't achieve anything in your life because you need to have the perfect idea for doing something enormous in your life. Without the God's call, you just live the life like an animal that gets through life on oxygen and food but your ultimate target is to be like the legends we will talk about below. The legends listened to the God's call on time and took action even if they were in the worst circumstances.

There is an activity, go back and think about your yesterday that what kind of thought you had most that day?

I am giving you space below to write down what you thought about for the most yesterday —

_____
_____
_____
_____
_____
_____
_____
_____

_____

Nothing is so dangerous to the progress of the human mind than to assume that our views of science are ultimate, that there are no mysteries in nature, that our triumphs are complete and that there are no new worlds to conquer.

~ Humphry Davy ~

Below are few examples from the website Wanderlust Worker which talks about few successful people who had listened to God's call.

Katy Perry

Most people know the name Katy Perry, but they don't the struggles that she faced. Perry started her career early in her life, dropping out of high school after freshman year in 1999 to pursue singing. Originally, she was a gospel singer, taking cues from her parents.

In 2001 Katy Perry released her first gospel album with Red Hill Records, which was commercially unsuccessful. After selling only 200 copies of her album, She kept signing the projects but kept failing in all. After being dropped from some major labels, you would think that Perry would have given up. She didn't. She was aware of her God's call. She said that she and strong feelings and intuitions for singing. She started working odd jobs and doing back-up vocals until she was signed to the newly-formed Capitol Music Group in 2006. It was there that she worked on her first huge hit single, "I Kissed a Girl". She used to listen to music while doing her work; she was into singing with all her beings. She made music her life even if she was facing hard time but she listened to her God's call that she had to build her career in Music itself.

J.K. Rowling

Rowling is one of the most inspirational success stories of our time. Many people simply know her as the woman who created Harry Potter. But, what most people don't know is what she went through prior to reaching popularity. Rowling's life was not tough; it was the toughest life which left her a diamond. She struggled tremendously.

In 1990, Rowling first had the idea for Harry Potter. She stated that the idea came "fully formed" into her mind one day while she was on a train from Manchester to London. She just saw a bird feather flying in the air and got an idea as a God's call to make a history by writing furiously.

In 1992 she moved to Portugal to teach English where she married to a man and had a daughter. Later her marriage ended in divorce and she moved to Edinburgh. At that time, she had three chapters of Harry Potter in her suitcase.

In 1995 all 12 major publishers rejected the Harry Potter script to get it published. But, it was a year later when a small publishing house, Bloomsbury, accepted it and provided her a very small £1500 advance. In 1997, the book was published with only 1000 copies, 500 of which were distributed to the local libraries.

In 1997 and 1998, the book won awards from Nestle Smarty's Book Prize and the British Book Award for Children's Book of the Year.

Today, Rowling has sold more than 400 million copies of her books, and is considered to be the most successful woman author in the United Kingdom. Whereas Rowling saw herself as a failure at that time. She was jobless, depressed, divorced, penniless, and with a dependent child but she didn't stop listening to her God's call. She got following her inner voice.

Bill Gates

Before he became one of the wealthiest men in the world, Bill Gates suffered many failures in business.

However, he didn't rely on his family of fate. His first business Traf-O-Data was a partnership between Gates, Paul Gilbert and Allen. The business aimed to create reports for roadway engineers from raw traffic data and but ended up as a failure.

Although Gates failed at his first business, it didn't discourage him from trying again. He didn't want to give up because the sheer notion of business intrigued him. He was cleverly able to put together a company that revolutionised the personal computing marketplace. Bill Gates himself says that the Microsoft was just an idea and to listen to an idea and cat upon it, it is just a task of yours. When Bill Gates heard his Silent Ring about the Microsoft and you all know just how successful that was for him.

Thomas Edison

When you hear the name of Edison, the picture of a bulb comes to your mind. It is said that Edison failed over 10,000 times to invent a commercially viable electric light bulb. But did that make him give up? No! Being a positive person, he always believed in seeing the light in the darkness. In the back of his mind, he always had the positivity and belief that he will succeed. He took it as God's call.

Once he was asked by a newspaper reporter if he felt like a failure and if he should give up, after having gone through thousands of failed attempts. To this, Edison simply stated, "Why would I feel like a failure? And why would I ever give up? I now know definitely over 9,000 ways an electric light bulb will not work. Success is almost in my grasp."

His company, GE, is still one of the largest publicly-traded firms in the world, continually innovating across virtually every spectrum. Sometimes it is good to be stubborn as Edison was for his successful invention.

My dear readers, I am presenting this unique chapter to make you more aware of your thoughts. Let us proceed with the opinion that planning, dedication, curiosity, the law of attraction, endeavours, everything works but if you don't have a strong reason, a valid thought, or the right concept, then you can't notch up anything. Let me try to clear your doubt with a short story:

Once upon a time, a farmer had a dog who used to sit by the roadside waiting for vehicles to come around. As soon as one came by, he would run down the road, barking and attempting to overtake it. One day a boy asked the farmer, "Do you think your dog is ever going to catch a car?" The farmer replied, "That is not what bothers me. What bothers me is what he would do if he ever caught one."

Many people in life behave like that dog who was pursuing an aimless aim or aim high by making life harder.

> *"Inch by inch, life's a cinch. Yard by yard, life's hard."*
>
> ~ John Bytheway ~

You will be getting God's call anytime. You need to be more cautious.

If you see something again and again,
If you think something again and again,
If you feel happy again and again while doing something,
If you do something which makes you say 'yes I love it',
If you behold the same good dream again and again,
Please don't ignore; that's God's call.
Think about it. Write it down. Act upon it.
God never comes to the earth or to your doorstep to tell you your target.
The Universe always gives us a signal.
See them. Observe them. Feel them.

Each and every person in the world receives the God's call but a lot of us ignore it because we don't focus on tiny things. Now please think about everything; may be in next second you are going to receive a God's call.

When you were born, there was no specific goal that you had. Neither were there any limitations. Goals and limitations which you now have, are set by yourself. We take birth without possessions, knowledge or belongings, and that is how we go. It is during our life here that we make sense of what we want our life to be. Some follow the rules and a set path ignoring God's call while other's pick up the slightest hint that they get from life and work on it. Missed opportunities have not made successful people who they are. Pick any autobiography and start reading it, and you will see umpteen examples of people paying attention to details, spotting God's call and acting upon them!

REAL PEOPLE, REAL STORIES

Hello from New York!!
I visited New York for 2 days in February 2016 and since then it became my dream city. After coming back home, I wanted to move to NY for work. Someday in December 2016 I read the visualisation session in the session and also read a couple of books which Vikas shared and got inspired by it. Since that day, I started visualising that I am sitting on a bench in front of the Brooklyn Bridge staring at the Manhattan skyline. I visualised this every day before sleeping and once during the day. In February 2017, I got an offer to work on a project in New York and had to leave Mumbai within a couple of days. I didn't even realise how and when this happened. I went and sat on the exact same bench which I used to visualise, looking at the Brooklyn Bridge and the beautiful Manhattan skyline. I am so grateful to Vikas and all the mentors from the group. It is because of their teaching and lessons that today I am working in New York as a freelancer. I don't know about the laws existing in the universe but I only know one thing that by attending this session I have got the power of my own life. I live my life the way I want. Vikas is amazing personality. He guides us spiritually,

emotionally and practically. The mentors are brilliant experts in their subjects.

Thank you Vikas for your support.

Mohit Pradhan
New York

CHAPTER TEN

Attracting Wealth and Manifesting Abundance

"If an egg is broken from outside force, Life ends. If broken by inside force, Life begins. Great things always begin from inside".

~ John Assraf ~

(A Recipe for Wealth and Abundance)

This was the most awaited session in my workshops as everyone wishes to have wealth and get the abundance in life. I kept taking session on this subject for some weeks and the attendants found so helpful and handy to use it. I also request my readers to go through the entire chapter. You will find magic at the end which you are unaware of it now. I went step by step like Cake… How to prepare the Cake? First thing comes to your mind is the recipe of the cake so I began my session like that…

Cake… Few foods evoke such a variety of meaning. For most people, cake is the culinary centerpiece of celebrations. Can you imagine a wedding or birthday party without it? Over the centuries cake has also been used as a metaphor for helpless poverty and propaganda of the French revolution. The popular expression — *you can't have your cake and eat it too* represents a limited belief system and a scarcity mindset.

For me, cake, and all baked goods really, symbolise pure abundance. Some of my fondest memories of childhood involve my mother's kitchen. I remember coming home daily to a new confection. My mother had what my sister and I call the baking gene. There was not a baked good she made that was not perfect and I suspect this had much to do with the sheer joy that baking brought her. Whatever I could wish for – devil's food cake, coconut cream pie, or a batch of the most decadent brownies - was waiting for my sister and me upon arrival. As I reflect back now, I realise that these moments in my mother's kitchen were my first introduction to the law of attraction.

When I think about it, the art of baking and the art of manifesting abundance have much in common. Both are governed by natural laws. If you go about things haphazardly, you will not get the results you desire. To manifest what is in your heart, you must bake from scratch. It can seem intimidating at first, but the right recipe and ingredients, combined with equal parts: desire, self-love, creativity, patience, resilience, and the willingness to get your hands dirty and take action can create the masterpiece you seek.

Put on your apron and join me and my friends in the Law of Attraction test kitchen. Let's peel back the icing on the cake and get some tasty morsels of what it really takes to manifest wealth and abundance. With enough effective practice, you can become the *magic* chef of your own life.

Meet the Master LOA Chefs

The fact that I'm calling these friends *master* would make them blush. They are normal, approachable people who desired to create for themselves an extraordinary life. And they succeeded *wildly*. I'm not just talking about their successful businesses, but the quality of their personal lives as well. Rich. Full. Abundant.

Jackie Ulmer Jackie is a legend in the direct sales industry and my first real mentor. In addition to being in the top 1% of earners in her industry, Jackie also runs a marketing and social media coaching business and is a frequent speaker at industry events. She has created a dream lifestyle for herself and her family.

Melanie Milletics Melanie is also a 7 figure earner in the direct sales and home business industry. She has created multiple streams of income through direct sales and in 2009 became the number one female earner worldwide in affiliate marketing.

Marty Keary Marty is a business magician. He co-owns several very successful businesses including restaurants, a wedding/banquet facility and the FocusMaster fitness empire. Marty is also an artist and author of the book Words From a Friend: A Daily Guide to a Purposeful Life.

Let's not sugar-coat it; nothing says LOVE like a self-rising cake.

"Cooking is like love. It should be entered into with abandon or not at all."

~ Harriet Van Horne ~

My favourite food themed movie is the international hit *Like Water for Chocolate*. The main character, Tita, is the most extraordinary cook. Each dish is infused with whatever emotion she is feeling as she cooks. If she is sad when she cooks, people cry as they eat her food. If she is happy, the diners experience joy. If she is feeling romantic…you get the picture. I thought it was sheer fantasy, but the law of attraction was really running the show. The behind the scenes preparation will determine what you manifest.

The preparation needed to manifest wealth and abundance in your life is much like self-rising flour. You have to create the lift for your own life. Others can give you inspiration and encouragement, but the kind of love you need to really move forward must come from your own heart. You do this by acts of self-love. This self-love permeates the batter of your world and is the base of your future masterpiece. It's simple, but requires the discipline to do it, especially when you don't *feel* worthy. There are three steps.

Calibrate the oven. *Gage Your Emotional Temperature and Vibration*

Baking requires you to pre-heat the oven. If the oven is not pre-set to the right temperature, baking time will not be accurate. Pre-heating the oven is similar to the inner work you need to do to program your mind for success.

Marty credits much of his success in business and in life to overcoming his limiting beliefs. A self-described "C" student, he is living proof that massive success does not come from grades in school, but from how well you train your mind. If you are willing to work daily on re-programming those negative thoughts, conquering your fears, and learning to forgive yourself and others you are off to a great start. That's not where it ends. Once you've got your emotional temperature, you need turn on your light so that others can benefit. According to Marty, "That's where the greatness lies."

Create your perfect recipe. *The Art of Setting Intentions and Deliberate Creation*

While the basics are the same for all baked goods- flour, liquid, leavening agent, everything else in the recipe is up to you. You create by default or intent. I first learned how to set intentions from Jackie Ulmer. I had no idea that was any different to setting goals. She taught me that by dreaming, visualising and believing in what you want you could achieve success.

Jackie has created an amazing lifestyle and a very successful business. She makes it seem effortless, but in reality the abundant life she has manifested is the result of carefully crafting her life by design. Her *secret* is to begin with the end in mind and makes every effort to align everything to that intention. An important part of that is aligning her belief. Jackie expects success and it shows.

Choose the best ingredients. Abundance Is Everywhere. Why Not Ask for the Best?

The Hidden Spark

You can get your ingredients from the dollar store, but why would you? Opportunities for abundance are all around you. You just have to open your eyes to see them. One of the ingredients I suggest you purchase is boldness. One of the boldest people I know is Melanie Milletics. This woman is pure fire energy.

Even when she doesn't "feel" like it, she has disciplined herself to radiate positive energy. A positive attitude attracts opportunities. She approaches life with a future mind; she has an **urgency** about her to be more, do more and have more. She's on a mission to bring others on this journey with her.

Although Melanie is super confident and positive, she believes over confidence can be a trap. If you are overestimating your abilities, then you are not improving your skills for success. Developing and improving your skills, so that you become an expert in your chosen industry can be considered among the best ingredients for wealth.

Into the mixer it goes…

"Cooking is the art of adjustment."

~ Jacques Pepin ~

When putting your ingredients into the mixer, you can't dump them in and turn on high speed. Well, you can, but you and your kitchen will be covered in flour. Instead you add the wet ingredients and mix slowly, adding the rest of the ingredients a little at a time until they are incorporated. Then, and only then, can you turn the speed to high. Creating wealth and abundance in your life abides by the same principle.

Are you still kneading dough by hand? *Don't Make Things Harder For Yourself – Keep It Simple Sweetie.*

For me, kneading dough is a dreaded task. It's exhausting. Imagine my glee when I discovered you can make great dough or crust in a food processor. Why work harder when you can work smarter?

Test. Evaluate. Measure your results. Melanie is a former high school science teacher, so it's no surprise that this is her motto. Like kneading bread dough, she believes we have to evaluate the effectiveness of what we are doing currently. We can't get stuck in what has worked in the past. Things are constantly changing. We are always growing and adjustments need to be made.

On the other hand, in the search for what's new and improved, we can over complicate matters, looking for the magic ingredient that will make everything easier. Sometimes tools help. Sometimes they don't. Melanie is an expert at using tools effectively. She is relentless about testing and evaluating every tool and method of operation in her business. Always looking for a way to be both more efficient and more effective, everything is evaluated; how can it be made better, how can this be simplified?

The truth about fast rising yeast. *Comparison Is a Dream Killer*

When using yeast, you have a choice — the regular variety or fast rising. In comparing the two, the difference lies in that the fast-rising yeast is the same except that it was packaged further in its development. Looks are deceiving, what you perceive as rapidly rising is actually something that has already been in development.

One ingredient that does not belong in your mix is comparisons. When you compare yourself to others you bring yourself into a negative place where you can never win. You block the good vibrations and energy and replace it with a smaller version of yourself. Marketing coach Jackie Ulmer, strongly urges her audience not show up as a cookie cutter version of someone else's model. Use your own unique voice. No one can tell your story. No one can live your dream.

All of us will experience comparisons or jealousy on our journey. A way I like to handle this is to examine why I am comparing or feeling jealous. What about that other person or situation do I admire or desire? Where do I feel like I am coming up short? I release those emotions and give thanks and appreciation for what that person brings to the world and me. Sometimes I'll keep this to myself; sometimes I'll send a note of appreciation. I then set an intention to re-create that in my own unique way if I still feel the desire.

There is something missing in the pumpkin pie! *Be Present. Focus. Go All In.*

I remember one Thanksgiving where I was making pumpkin pie. My small kitchen was full of the multitude of dishes I was cooking for the feast and I had four sons under the age of ten running through the kitchen. It was total chaos. I had the pumpkin pie filling in the mixer, another dish cooking on the stove that needed my attention and yet another pie in the oven that needed to come out. After eating a beautiful meal, I proudly served the pies. That's when my son yelled, Mom, there is something wrong with the pumpkin pie!" Sure enough, in all the chaos, I forgot to add the sugar. I was completely distracted and the result was something short of the mark.

Laser focus is how to bring your intentions into fruition. If you are not fully present and focused on what you are doing at the given moment, you may miss what is necessary. Whether he's holding an event at one of his gyms, giving a couple a beautiful wedding experience, or building a piece of furniture from reclaimed wood, Marty is all in! I can tell this from the pictures and the joy in which he shares his adventures with his friends on Facebook. Marty talks frequently about the power of the present moment and believes only in the present do we have the ability to change our course. When you balance many plates, the extent to which you develop your ability to focus can be the deciding factor in how far you go.

Is there such a thing as an easy bake oven?

"Baking may be regarded as science, but it's the chemistry between the ingredients and the cook that give desserts life."

~ Anna Olson ~

My first encounter with baking lit a fire under me, literally. I was five years old and had a friend over to play. It was my intention (the first one I can consciously remember) to enjoy a sumptuous feast fit for two princesses. There was one problem; I couldn't find any grown-ups to help me. I was determined to manifest my idea, so off I went into the pantry with a chair to reach the ingredients. I remember my friend watching as if I were a magician, slathering the peanut butter on the bread and sprinkling the raisons on top. There was just one last detail to make it perfect, some time in the "easy bake" oven.

Off my little masterpieces went into the oven. This was not the type of oven like kids have today. It was half the size of a regular stove and had no timer. Off we went to the playroom, quickly forgetting the food. A while later we remembered the food only because of the smell of burning peanut butter toast.

The art of manifesting your creation is like my experience with the easy bake oven. You shouldn't expect great results if you are not willing to monitor the process. Expect, then inspect; not set and forget. It's a balance between trusting the process and checking for doneness. Also, realise mishaps will happen and you need to keep going. One beautiful lesson my mother taught me from this was, to get back up and try again after failing. The oven was toast, but when I was ready she bought me another.

Here are three tips for making the baking process easier:

Keep the oven door shut! *The Law of Detachment and Learning to Trust*

Once you've pre-heated the oven and mixed your ingredients, its time to place them in the oven. This is the *incubation* and rising period. Opening the oven door will drop your temperature by 25 degrees each time. If you want to check on your progress before the timer sounds, use the light inside. Another crucial time in baking is the cooling down time after baking before unveiling your masterpiece.

When you put your life plan into the universe's oven, you trust that the oven will bake your cake. The universe will bake whatever cake you put into at whatever temperature you set. If you have the right emotions and mindset, with powerful intentions you should be good to go. You just have to TRUST. You need to know that everything will fall into place so you can detach yourself from the outcome. You need to believe with your whole self that these things will come to pass at the right time.

Jackie Ulmer recommends the 90 day plan. The idea is to commit any major course of action for 90 days before re-evaluating. This prevents you from continually opening the oven door, reducing your emotional temperature and second guessing yourself.

Create a test kitchen atmosphere. *Reviewing Your Day and Week with Intention*

Every plan needs review. You are committing to a major course of action for 90 days, but small reviews and tweaks are needed daily and weekly. Jackie's approach to reviewing your day is intuitive. Before bed, she encourages people to let go of what happened that day and to ask empowering questions. What went right today? What could I do better tomorrow? What am I grateful for? These questions give an evaluation of your progress and not where you've fallen short.

Don't panic if the soufflé falls. *The Law of Sufficiency and the Art of Bouncing Back*

Soufflés can be intimidating to create. One wrong move and it can fall flat. Thankfully life is not like that. It's all in how you frame tings. Scoop out the contents, put some whipped cream on it and call it *rustic*.

No one I personally know is better at bouncing back from adversity than Melanie. She's come back twice from nothing to recreate her 7 figure empire. She credits this to three things: faith, mindset, and taking action. She has faith that God has and will continue to provide everything she needs for success. There is no wavering in that belief. She also has faith in her ability to make it happen and this comes from the way she chooses to think. To get out of feeling bad about a situation, she goes back to the basics and works on retraining her brain for success heavily. This allows her to see failure as a learning opportunity. To look for opportunities in everything, to be flexible in your thinking and possibly come up with a new plan. Finally, Melanie is a firm believer that action is where the money is. You must take daily consistent action on **revenue generating** activities.

Have Your Cake and Eat It All

"This was why she enjoyed baking. A good dessert could make her feel like she'd created joy at the tips of her fingers. Suddenly, the people around the table were no longer strangers. They were friends and confidantes, and she was sharing with them her magic."

~ Marissa Meyer, Heartless ~

True wealth comes from relationships. In the end, you cannot take any material goods with you into the next life. It's what you pour into people that will last. It's the legacy you leave. Your relationship with others is the great multiplier. The wealth and abundance you hope to truly experience is the result of the quality of your relationships with others, the quality of your relationship with yourself, and the quality of the network you build.

The creation of their uncommon lifestyles has allowed each of my friends to be able to spend the kind of time with their family that most people only dream of. They've traveled the world with their children; they've been available for school events. Recently all three of my friends have been able to be there for their ageing parents when they really needed them. Isn't that where the real wealth is?

The Joy of Baking. *How gratitude and giving back create abundance in your life*

One trait my friends have in common is the practice of giving back. They incorporate others into their plans and spread light and joy. They take pleasure in showing others the path they've taken to achieve abundance. They also find ways to help good causes they believe in. One mantra all the successful people I know utter is, "Be a giver and not a taker."

Another common element is the daily practice of gratitude. Every day, without fail, I will get through my friends feed a post of something Marty, Jackie and Melanie are grateful for. Whether it's a business triumph, a happy family moment or just something beautiful they see outdoors, there always something positive and uplifting coming from their heart to the world. Daily. I know they have their private, more extensive gratitude lists, but I love this public expression. It says to the world, "This is how I am choosing to show up today." It also inspires others to do the same.

One last observation is that cultivating the habits of gratitude and giving back help create the wealth and abundance you are seeking. It's a self-fulfilling cycle. To get you have to give. You have to start right where you are now.

Bake sale or gourmet patisserie? *Be Confident in the Value of Who You Are and What You Provide*

Key to creating wealth is how abundant you feel about yourself. Are you valuing yourself at bake sale prices or do you consider yourself to be worthy of more? This is all about the relationship you create with yourself. It's about how much time and money you are willing to spend on personal growth. Start where you are, but be willing to invest more into you as you grow. This is called levelling up.

How you value yourself is made evident by your surroundings and the people you spend time with. Always choose to be around the best quality you can.

Your strategies for wealth creation should be a reflection of who you are. This includes marketing and pricing strategy for business owners. (For those employed this would be how you position yourself in your company.) If you don't charge what you are worth, this lack of confidence comes across in everything you do. First, you need to be certain of the quality of the product or service you are providing. If you have a quality in what you are offering, but still lack the confidence to ask for your value then you need to look at the underlying cause. Fear. What is it exactly that you are afraid of? It's time to recalibrate your mind.

Enjoy the dessert buffet. *Limitless Thinking and Manifesting Multiple Streams of Income*

When I think of limitless thinking, I think of Marty Keary. I remember Mr. Murtha's senior high marketing class. The class was asked what kind of business we wanted to own. Marty said he wasn't sure which kind, but that he wanted several businesses. Ask and ye shall receive. Today Marty's empire includes a catering business, a wedding facility, and two new restaurants are opening this year. His fitness business is expanding. He has the time to create his art. Marty will tell you he didn't do it alone. He believes that success comes from relationships and works with a team of co-owners and employees that create the vision with him.

One key is to look for others to help you on your way to success. You need to be confident that the right people will be brought into your life at the right time. Another key point is focus. Before adding another business stream, you need to make sure what you already have is going strong. One layer needs to be upright on it's own before you add the next layer.

So there you have it. Great lessons from LOA master chefs. I haven't given you theory, but three real life examples of people I personally know that are truly experiencing the life of their dreams. Manifesting wealth and abundance in your life is not easy. You can't get there just by wishing, you have to follow a basic recipe and take smart action. Now its time for you to get creating. What delicious things will you begin to manifest in your life?

REAL PEOPLE, REAL STORIES

Hello friends! I am a firm believer in - whatever happens, it happens for a reason. The day when I got added to the workshop created by Vikas, I thought it's going to be yet another group. But I am extremely happy and thankful because I have had so many learning from the workshop conducted by you and the other mentors. It has changed my life, the way I think, the way I do things, the way I work, everything !!!

I am so very grateful to you Vikas because there are very few people on this planet earth who like helping people without their interest and greed and you are one of them. I love helping people and I relate my profession to it as well. I grow when my people grow! I loved the session "The Imaginiotic Therapy" I use it as a weapon to create my lovely world. All mentors are great.

Thank you so much!

Akanksha Chauhan
Bengaluru, India

I am very stubborn person in my life and I used to claim that no one could change me at all specially my attitude towards my life. I liked to live the life the way I wanted but sometimes I used to face problems which ailed me a lot but I took this workshop lightly because I used to think myself as a learned person but the real magic happened when I read the story of one member in the workshop that she had got a complete control over anxiety so I also thought of taking help of the sessions. The meditation session helped me a lot to get rid of anxiety. In short I must say that each second, minute, hour, day, week, month has become blessings to me. Thank you so much for changing me Vikku and all the mentors.

Rucha Goel
NewDelhi, India

CHAPTER ELEVEN

THE LAW OF ECHO

What are words? How do you speak? Why do you speak? When do you speak? What makes you speak? Here are some questions connected to my chapter *The Law of Echo*. This chapter will represent everything here including the answers beautifully.

It is said, "Spoken words never die." This is the reason why ancient time people were cursed by the saints and monks and at that exact time, their words used to come true. One of the Indian epic *Ramayana* stated that, "In this childhood, once Lord Hanumana tried to disturb some saints while playing on the trees with his friends, he was cursed by them that in the time of need, he would forget his divine strength. After many years, when Lord Rama was in search of goddess Sita, had approached Lord Hanumana was asked to find Goddess Sita in Ravan's Lanka (now SriLanka) as he was known to be the strongest of all lords. At that time, Lord Hanuma was suddenly unable to fly all the way to SriLanka but later he was reminded of his unlimited power by his companion Nal and Neel and then he got his power back."

This above story tells you that saints' curses worked throughout Hanuman's life until he was reminded. That is why it is said that, *words, prayers, wishes, curse work all the time.*

As the old saying goes, *"in space, no one can hear you scream,"* without air there is no sound.

But if that's true, what was space physicist Don Gurnett talking about when he stated at a NASA press conference on Sept. 2013 that he had heard '*some weird sounds in the space like some people were speaking?*'. Although many questions were raised over that interview but it proves one thing that, "The spoken words exist for years."-

You speak when you need to convey your message to someone. Generally you take help from the words in a particular language. The language does not matter because I am Indian so I can understand Hindi language very well but if any other person speaks to me in his language, I wouldn't understand that but I may get his emotions, expression, feelings etc. It means that you do require emotions in your words, not language. When you speak, while gesticulating with your hands in the air, your action creates your mental mood. Whenever you feel good or bad, you always speak and while speaking, your words judge your mental status. This is similar to what I had mentioned in the previous chapter, that to manifest something in your life, you need to focus on your feelings especially good one.

> *"The right word spoken at the right time can make all the difference in building people up. Choose well."*
>
> ~ Michael Hyatt ~

The *law of echo* means the power of spoken words. While speaking and choosing your words, you attract the same things in your life by sending out the vibrations. I have observed many people making fun of others, backbiting, taunting, insulting, arguing etc but they don't know that indirectly there are attracting the same emotions in their own life. They are inviting the negative energy or mishaps in their life. There are many laws working in the universe like "You must give to receive". If you want to have prosperity in your life then talk about prosperity, talk about happiness, money, good health and wealth rather than pulling someone's leg or poking nose in others' business because if you do this to others then you, yourself need to be ready to face this.

You have only one teacher: Your words you speak. Your words build you and destroy you. The words you speak which affects your conscious and subconscious minds. The more positive words you speak for yourself, the more your subconscious mind gets activated. Your subconscious mind makes you work towards your goal. Science and spirituality both work here. If I talk about the secret behind the law of echo, science does work here. Sports psychology says, "Shouting helps you bring to the victory." The best example of the *law of echo* is the Rio Olympics Games, 2016, a major international multi-sport event was held in Rio de Janeiro, Brazil, from 5 August to 21 August 2016. On 19th August, 2016, the final badminton women's single match was held between PV Sindhu from India and Carolina Marin from Spain. They both struggled a lot to win the match as it was a neck to neck match. At one point Sindhu was ahead but after a while Carolina came back, and it went so on. It was like a win-win situation for both and neither lost the hope of winning the match. Sindhu was ahead in the first round but Carolina Marin began to use the technique which is called **the law of echo**. She started saying *yes* aloud, every time she played a shot. She would tell herself, "I am doing great. I am nearer to the win, I am overtaking, I am not tired."

If you watch on YouTube, you will find that there was totally unique technique being used by Carolina Marin. Sindhu made all Indian proud by making remarkable efforts whereas Carolina made history by winning the Gold medal.

Now the question poised here, how did the *law of echo* work during the game?

Playing games or chasing goals, both are same because in both, you are in the hunger of success. But by only working hard you won't be able to notch up the goal since concentration and mental balance are as important as winning the match. When you talk to yourself, your inner power gets activated. You meet yourself inside of you. You start recognising yourself. *Plato* says, **"When the mind is thinking it is talking to yourself or itself.** Once you get giving positive affirmations to yourself, it means you explore yourself for higher betterment, for the bigger challenges, to enable your mental strength. You adjust yourself to the toughest point which seemed to be difficult to you."

Self–Talk:- Self-talk is the best remedy and always recommended by the mind psychologists to be used when you feel down because the self-talk technique enhances your hidden energy, it removes your mental blockages and lethargy that you feel. Self talk motivates you to take creative steps towards your aim.

Mirror-Talk:- Mirror-talk is also considered to be the best therapy as you see yourself the way you want because the mirror does not lie, it reflects what you are. Whatever you speak in front of the mirror, it reflects back to you and shows who you are going to be!

You may take help from these following positive affirmations to use the law of echo -

1. I am a winner.
2. I am destined to win.
3. I am successful.
4. I am a champion.
5. I live for this.
6. I am able
7. Yes! I am doing great.
8. Yes! I can do it.
9. I was born to do this.
10. I succeed with ease.

If I talk about the spirituality in speaking the suitable words or using the law of echo, here is tale which describes you to be more cautious about using the words. Once, Kumbhakarana (Lord Ravana's) went to bushy forest for the worship to impress the lord Brahma (creator of the world according to Hindu mythology). When lord Bhrahma was pleased by

The Hidden Spark

him, he appeared to know what wish would Kumbhakarana want to be fulfilled by him. Kumbhakarana was about to wish to have victory over his sleep; that he will sleep only one day evert six months. But by mistaken he blurted, "Oh Lord, bless me the boon of six months of sleep and one day of staying awake to eat and meet my family". Lord Bhrahma granted the wish and Kumbhakarana was left disappointed for having wished for the wrong wish!

Overall moral of the story is that you must be aware of your words while speaking because words be granted by the universe.

The *law of echo* presents the power of your words so you can use it as a weapon in your life because awareness does not cost but provides you the best result as you want.

Every word has energy. Whatever you speak gives you energy. Have you ever seen labourers talking? They generally use abusive language or bad words for themselves or for others and what is their status? They always remain in poverty. Have you ever listened to any businessman's talking? They always speak in a gentle voice, use specific words and even they speak about their health and wealth so they blossom in the field of business. "Everyone knows to speak but fewer know what to speak".

Just remember one thing, whatever is in your mind, echoes into the aura around it. If you are trying hard to get some work done, but in your mind, you have already accepted defeat, they defeat is yours. But if at that moment, along with hard work, if you are telling yourself that you can do it, there is nothing that can stop you, etc, the positivity will seep through your aura and give your action a bold push. You don't have to believe it just because I am saying so. I urge you to try this for yourself. Next time you are faced with a challenging situation where you have to work hard to come out of it, try telling yourself positive things. Reassure yourself that you can do it and only you can do it. Notice the change in your attitude and force in completing the task at hand. You will emerge successful and that is what will make you a winner!

****

REAL PEOPLE, REAL STORIES

Hello friends! I have a million success stories after attending the workshop. I don't want to tell you about my past mishaps because I don't want to recall everything bad which happened to my life. Now I believe in my positive magical life. I have my own business. I earn a very huge amount of money every month. I have a very beautiful family. I have a very good quality of friends. I have become noted among my friends circle by my positive attitude. All respects me a lot. I find beauty even in muddy water; I have fallen in love with myself and my life. There is no shortage of anything in my life. I have become abundance in my life. Vikas aapne yeh kya kar diya muje ki muje meri life me sirf positivity hi dikhti hai (Vikas, you have cast a magic upon me), the great mentors like Rosie, Karen, Chole, Cora, Hiral and you are wonderful. Thank you so much for making my life beautiful. This session is so priceless that Vikku has not charged us at all. You guys are God's angel. Thank you, thank you, thank you, thank you, thank you, thank you...

Kalpana Bhatiya
Dubai

Please do not show pity on me because I am blessed in my life. I am 34 years engineer. I lost my husband three years back. I did not lose my husband, I have lost everything. I could trust on animals but I could not count on people after my husband's demise. Today I am alive and better due to some friends in my life. Having left all bad experiences behind, I would like to say that this workshop helped me a lot to overcome the depression. I loved one statement which was spoken by Vikas bhai in the session that "Only you can save yourself". I thought about that sentence several times. I realized that I would have to live to show the people who were pointing and taunting at me. I swam across the ocean and saved myself. Today I am earning a handsome salary and I have peace in my life. Yeah! I am aloof in my life but the teachings of this session are always with me and I got a brother like Vikku and all the mentors as my guides and all the attendants as my friends. Now I have a big family with me. My husband is always with me, he is within me.

Thank you so much all of you for being with me!

Shweta Parashar
Pune, Maharashtra

CHAPTER TWELVE

VISUALIZATION TO MANIFESTATION

"Visualise the most amazing life imaginable to you. Close your eyes and see it clearly. Then hold the vision for as long as you can. Now place the vision in god's hands and consider it done."

~ Marianne Williamson ~

Visualisation costs nothing; it is free for all because it is one of the finest and most powerful tools which you are provided by the universe. Have you ever observed that most of the successful people spend their time alone, they take time in taking decisions and understating the concepts and listening to others first? By one of the article, it reveals the secret that they take time so because they visualise the ultimate results, they keep their mind engaged in visualising the outcome of the conversation or a business deal. Visualisation is a technique to use it in fulfilling your aims, bringing your dreams into reality, making your wishes comes true, removing negativity, allowing the law of attraction work, activating your subconscious mind, becoming mentally, physically, financially, spiritually, and emotionally stronger. Visualisation is used by millions of people especially by the top most successful people in the world.

In fact, you all have this outstanding power, but most of you have never been taught to use it effectively.

The athletes use it. Rich people use it. All kinds of people use it. The peak performers in all fields use it. This technique not only helps you achieve your goals but also helps you stay away from all negativities and issues. Visualisation means seeing the goal as already achieved in your mind's eye (Pineal Gland). Visualisation is effective because it activates the power of your subconscious mind which opens the doors of health, wealth, happiness, prosperity and fulfilment of your goals to you. It is a step that you take to fulfil your dreams and manifestation is the outcome of your visualisation. To visualise something is as easy as having piece of cake but persistency is the key important as the universe loves the consistency in sending out the vibration.

Here are I am explaining some more tips about visualisation and manifestation —

Becoming Visual

"I see trees of green, red roses too. I see them bloom for me and you. And I think to myself what a wonderful world." — Louie Armstrong, from the song "What a Wonderful World".

Apple has a slogan — Think Different. Most of the readers of this book already think different or aspire to. I'd like to challenge you to SEE different. Seeing different was the first lesson my mother taught me on how to dream. I was taught not to see things at face value but to instead see things as they could be. When I look at something I see the potential fulfilled as well as the reality.

Tip to follow :- Seeing different can be difficult. A way to train yourself to do this is by observing something and then describing it. Write or draw your object with as much detail as possible. Do this again, but change the description to include how you actually want to see it.

Becoming Sensual

It feels like the world disappears around us." ~ Natashia Beddingfield, in the song Touch

This isn't about being sexy, although putting the law of attraction into practice is sexy. What I mean by being sensual is that you need to bring the fullness of your senses into the equation. This is where you create in vivid detail, the vision of what you desire to become your reality. Let the ordinary world disappear and let each detail come to life. What do you see, hear, taste, smell, and feel? What are you feeling and doing?

Tip to follow :- If you have a difficult time bringing sensuality into the equation, try this exercise to develop sensual awareness. Too often as we rush through our days, we lose this ability. I want you to slow down and experience your senses fully as you go about your day. Close your eyes. Notice how something feels against your skin. What flavours do you taste with each bite? Can you distinguish the spices? As you walk outside can you feel the wind? What do you hear?

Becoming Aware

One step beyond creating a sensual vision is creative visualisation. This is all about feeling different. Creative visualisation takes it up one notch by integrating the feelings you are feeling as you see yourself achieving your vision. By using your positive emotions as triggers, you will attract more of that into your life. A key part to experience this is to get yourself into an alpha state of mind before you start the visualisation process.

Tip to follow :- The alpha state is a brain wave state that is highly conducive to dreams, mediations, daydreaming, reprogramming the subconscious, and creative visualisation. You can bring yourself down to this level from your active conscious mind through mediation and binaural beats. I use both. This is a topic worth further exploration, as there are many techniques and tools. You need to search to find the best fit for you.

Becoming Your Avatar

This step involves creating an avatar of WHO you are when your vision is manifested. What does the YOU of your vision wear, eat, and enjoy? Once you've created your avatar, you need to become the avatar, at least some of the time. This not only includes setting goals and taking action step toward them, but you need to take intuitive action on your desires. This sensual action steps add a tangible, tactile element to the visualisation process. This is where you DO different. Where you play "pretend."

Tip to follow:- Let's say, your desire is to travel or move to a foreign country. In addition to taking practical action steps towards this goal, you also take sensual actions. You wear a few items of clothing from the country. Enjoy the cuisine on a regular basis. Watch their movies. Enjoy their art. Listen to the music. Immerse yourself in the physical experience of it as much as you can from where you are.

Becoming a True Believer

"I believe in the lost possibilities you can see."

~ Christina Perry, from the song I Believe ~

There is a famous saying that many Law of Attraction practitioners disagree with – "You have to see it to believe it." They say that believing comes before seeing and that is partially true. It's a self-fulfilling cycle. Once you see different and develop a sensual vision, you then internalise the vision through the power of your emotions coupled with visualisation. By the time you've taken sensual actions to become your avatar, this process has worked its way into you at the soul level. You are now BEING different. In every moment, in every decision we manifest our future. In every moment, the choice is yours.

Tip to follow :- Choose gratitude over indifference every day. Choose faith over fear. Choose positivity over negative thoughts. Choose possibilities over defeat.

Visualisation helps you to manifest your dreams once you start doing this technique.

"Visualisation is the process of creating pictures in your mind of yourself enjoying what you want. When you visualise, you generate powerful thoughts and feelings of having it now. The law of attraction then returns that reality to you, just as you saw it in your mind."

~ Rhonda Byrne ~

****

REAL PEOPLE, REAL STORIES

Namaste! Amazingly and wonderful changes you (all mentors) all made in my life, yes!! I can say its life changing session. Heartfelt thank you to my dearest friend Vikas for starting such a session to help millions of aimless people providing us all miraculous chance to learn and turn out to be the best version of ourselves life has always been beautiful to me through many ups and downs. But after being a part of this workshop, I learned to explore my hidden spark and my qualities. I am now aware about my potential and each and every session made me more aware about my abilities. I have become fully focused person in my life. I meditate everyday and attract the thing I want and I feel peace in my life. I loved the session "Question\Answer" which cleared many doubts.

Thank you so much

Kavita Rathi
Surat, Gujarat

Success story of the girl who tried a lot to make herself nobody to somebody. Nothing different from others, tried so many things and failed again, I tried again but failed again but I never quit. Somewhere I have complete faith that I am the God's angle and he has wonderful plan for me. I was struggling in my life and carrier. Suddenly a person came in my life. I have learnt many things from him. Somehow our vibrations matched and started being a very good friends. I have strongly started believing in the law of attraction and many more things in his guidance. He is the one who just spreading his wisdom to all and was not aware about many people implementing those in their life and getting success and I am one of them. I love him a lot because he is a true mentor, true friend, true guider and a best version of human being. His efforts are remarkable. He connected with all over the world to give us the best. Thank you so much Vikas Trivedi for being one of my best friend. I am giving my best to get retired from the hard work in an early age so that I can go on the world tour with my family. I am fully focused on my business. The mentors from different countries also played a very great role in our lives.

                Gratitude and love!
                           Shrankhala Tomar
                           New Delhi, India

CHAPTER THIRTEEN

NO HURRIES FOR THE WORRIES

In this modern era, people are after their dreams and do whatever they can to bring into real world, but they forget about feeding the mind. As you might come to know about the mind's power in achieving our goals.

Stress:-
Stress has become a common element in our day to day life style. As a society, you are bombarded with ongoing activities and tasks: going to work, cooking, cleaning, family, friends, gym and much, much more. Stress impacts us in various ways; emotionally, physically and spiritually. Mentally, overloading yourself with repetitive and pervasive thoughts can overload your mind causing you to stress out. Spiritually, being stressed places distance between the focus of your worries and the focus of your higher self. At a physical level your body when stressed produces elevated amounts of cortisol hormones; when your cortisol levels are high this impacts your learning and memory. The brain and nervous system are impacted by stressors in many ways. For one, having stress releases different hormones like epinephrine, and norepinephrine which cause the heart rate to increase, blood pressure to increase, breathing rate to increase, and blood sugar to increases as well. Dealing with too

much stress can cause feelings of nervousness, nausea, diarrhea, chronic back, neck pain, trembling, hives, and insomnia. As you may note the physical symptoms of stress should motivate us to manage our stress.

Did I save my work onto the computer drive? Do I know what time piano lessons are? When is the water bill due? These are examples of stressful thoughts; in essence you create these thoughts that stress you out. Similarly, you have the potential to create the thoughts that create a sense of serenity, order and balance in your life. Thoughts like, "All is well, I can schedule time for that task, I will strategize for that goal, I will call her back on my lunch break, I plan to complete this task by this time" you can always tell ourselves words that encourage you and keep you on task in your day to day activities.

Although routines keep you comfortable, routines can also stress you, you may repress the stress of the idea "I dislike my job but I am comfortable there and do not want to stress out finding another job", or you may repress the stress of being in a difficult relationship because you are repressing the stress that comes from a break up. Repression of stress is very common, you can decide to pretend that stress is not present in a situation but this will only magnify it. It is better for stress to be "aired" out in the open, consciously ask yourself, is this situation, person or thing stressing me out? You must be willing to be open about your stress and learn to identify when you are feeling stressed and with whom you feel stressed around. Awareness is the first step to identify stress but it takes action to create a change in consciousness. Your human experience would not be the same without the stress involved. Think and tell yourself, "I am stressed but I know how to relax myself, all is well" and so it is.

Essentially, having a daily, weekly and monthly calendar can keep you aligned with your every day responsibilities and potentially decrease our stress; make sure you schedule time for your preferred stress free activities as well. Stress does not discriminate between cultures, genders, religions or political backgrounds, stress impacts everyone, however, you all cope with stress differently. A wise man once told me "anything that has value in your life will stress you." This statement resonated with me, indeed stress allows you to act upon that which you care including ourselves. Paul J. Rosch M.D. states "I think the single most important point you can make about stress is that in most cases it's not what's out there that's the problem, it's how you react to it." Your attitude towards your everyday stressful tasks is what determines how you feel in that moment. You can choose to feel confident in your ability to perform the task or you can fear not being able to go through with the task. Do you recall having assignment due with your boss? or a project due to your teacher? More than likely you had a due date, in a way, stress urges us to act in a timely fashion, certainly, due dates keep our efforts in a timeline; however, due dates also provide that extra stress. Therefore, you must be conscious in how you are interpreting our current situation, timeline and tasks, if we see something as difficult and stressful, it will be so, if we perceive a task as easy and productive, it will be so. Plan your tasks according to the time available and remember not to overbook yourself.

There are certainly moments in life that one can be stressed like organizing your wedding, having a family member pass away, losing a job, these events can possibly inhibit symptoms of stress. You all experience stressful moments in life, stress is indeed a human condition and should be honored as such. What I mean by honored is to be acknowledged, to be in the open and to be accepted. As you accept your life with stress you will honor it and you will open the gates of what I call the "Relaxation Paradise" this is where you find your internal sanctuary. How you feel internally is everything in life, it is true that man cannot buy happiness for this is a state of mind. Indeed, you need to create this consciousness with your whole hearted effort because it is not created for you. Internally you must be aware of how you feel in order to identify when you are stressed. Once you have identified you are stressed the trick is to identify an activity that will help you cope through the stressful moment or thought. Remember that although stressful thoughts come into your mind they do not stay, unless you decide so of course. Now, that you have identified you are experiencing a stressful moment you can plan on going to Relaxation Paradise.

Relaxation Paradise

The ability for the human body to relax and the mind to find serenity is a practice that takes conscious effort. Creating your own "Relaxation Paradise" will require you have knowledge of the self. Let's start by identifying the senses of your preference. The five human senses touch, taste, smell, auditory and visual can all be used to help relax the body and mind. During my time teaching parenting classes I reminded parents that it was important to make time for relaxation activities on a daily basis. I also reminded them how stress impacted their parenting skills and patience with their children.

Aromatherapy:-

Taking a journey with aromatherapy to relaxation paradise is delightful. I recall as a child smelling my food prior to eating it. As an adult, I enjoy smelling aromas that relax me. Aromatherapy is the use of essential oils for the benefit of our body and mind. The extraction of essential oils has been used since the times of ancient Egypt; the oils were used to embalm the dead. Countries like China started using essential oils as mood enhancers. It was French chemist Rene Maurice Gattefosse that described the use of the essential oil as "healing". One of my favorite essential oils is lavender which I use on my pillow at night to sooth me into my sleeping mode. I also dilute my oils in water in spray my office consistently, especially if I have an upcoming assignment with a due date and I'm feeling stressed. At times, I also use aromas of essential oils prior to meditating; this helps my mind relax as I enter what I call the "zen zone". For me, being in the zen zone is best described as the notion of timelessness where I am not worried about the time, about work, about cooking, I am worry free completely. The use of aromatherapy has impacted me profoundly as it has allowed me to enjoy the aromas that soothe me internally. Essential oils are relaxing for the body and mind allowing us to decrease our stress. The effect that aromas have on the mind is powerful. Just think of the opposite, the smell of a dirty diaper or a trashcan and how it impacts your mood; similarly, when positive aromas impact your nose your mood shifts positively. Aromatherapy can be used as a tool to balance our daily stressors.

Reiki :-

Reiki can be used as an experience that leads us to relaxation paradise. Reiki is an ancient Spiritual technique used for healing the human energy field. Honorable Master Mikao Usui was the founder of Reiki which originated in Japan. It is important to clarify that Reiki is not a religion; however, it is a Spiritual practice, "Rei" meaning Gods wisdom or Higher Power and "Ki" meaning life force energy. Using the higher power and life force energy to heal and restore energetic balance to ourselves and others is what Reiki Masters do. Reiki uses the energy in the natural environment to restore the energetic balance to the recipient. The Reiki practitioner or Master uses their hands, prayer and intuitive guidance during a Reiki healing session. Reiki is placed on the energetic epicenters of our Aura known as chakras; as well as certain areas of our body. For the past four years I have been providing Reiki to people of my community. There are many misconceptions about Reiki that I would like to clarify. Reiki does not claim to cure anything; it is not a replacement therapy. You do not have to be ill to benefit from Reiki, you can always benefit from a little boost of life force energy no matter your age. Nicola Tesla believed that energy was everywhere and accessible at all times and as a Reiki practitioner I can confirm this. Energy is all around all the time, just like sunlight during the day and moonlight during the night. Reiki gives us the opportunity to relax during treatment and after; I encourage you to add Reiki as a relaxation activity to help decrease your stress.

Meditation:-

Internal conversations with my higher self provide direction in my life. I have learned to respect the voice within for it has guided me to my greatest good. Your consciousness is always striving to improve your relationship with yourself and others. Meditation is a Spiritual technique that allows you to connect with your higher self and the Universe. The benefits of meditation can also be derived from scientific research; according to studies, people who meditate tend to have better sleeping patterns, improved mental clarity, focus, creativity, and a better ability to cope with stressors. Spiritually, meditating amplifies your ability to be present in the moment, it increases your sensibility, patience and empathy; ultimately, it allows you to have better relationship with yourself and others.

The practice of meditation is holistic in nature for it is benefiting the body, mind and Spirit. Practicing a technique that provides benefits on all areas of your being has the potential to impact how you think and feel. Meditation has the power to change perspectives and allows you to think on a conscious level. It is best to practice meditation consistently; meditation can be incorporated to your daily schedule of activities. Meditation in the morning may lead you mind to organize and maximize our day; it can provide clarity on decisions and problem resolutions. Meditation in the afternoon may help alleviate the stress accumulated during your work day. Meditation during the night may help you fall asleep better, especially if you are experiencing insomnia. Mediation can be done at any time of the day as long as you are consciously participating in it. For you to practice meditation effectively you need to identify your meditation preferences, your meditation script and your mental and Spiritual focus.

Ask yourself about,

Meditation Preferences :-
What is my favourite meditative pose?
Do I enjoy meditating sitting down?
Lying down?
On the couch?
On a chair?
In the shower?
In nature?
By my desk?

Meditation Script

Close your eyes,
Let your thoughts come in,
Become aware of your thought
Visualize the thought
Place the though in a bubble
Let the bubble go
Let the thought go
Let all thoughts go
One by one
As they come
Until your mind is free

Mentally, when we are in a meditative state of mind…

You are able to identify your emotions
You are able to organise your feelings
You are able to feel compassion for others and the self
You are able to empathise with your heart
You are able to be open minded to new possibilities
You are able to think of new problem resolutions
You are able to think clearly about your actions
You are able to visualise your goals

Spiritually, when we are in a meditative state of mind…

You can access your higher self
You have an opportunity
To inquire within
The divine
To receive feedback and direction
To connect with all
The collective consciousness
And the Universe

Mediation, Reiki and Aromatherapy are all techniques that can lead you to relaxation paradise. These techniques focus on the development of your body, mind and Spirit. They are what I call the sacred trinity of activities for the soul. Your immune system functions better when your stress is low then when your stress is high. Research has confirmed that stress impacts your overall health and your attitude towards stress has the potential to impact on how you perceive your daily stressors. Therefore, the more positive your perception about your stressors, the better the outcome for your health; this is especially true in mental health. George Shambaugh M.D. believes "stress is not something you can beat but a force you can turn to your advantage." Stress can give you the opportunity to engage in activities that restore your balance and by participating in holistic activities you allow yourself to grow as human beings. Stress allows you to act in a timely fashion and ultimately stress allows you to engage in a deeper relationship with ourselves by looking within and getting to ourselves better. Indeed many would like to walk away from stress, however it is not humanly possible, the next best thing you can do for yourself and those around you is to make sure you develop the tools necessary to manage your stressors. This will lead you to a more happy and balanced life.

REAL PEOPLE, REAL STORIES

Namaste! I am a staunch follower of The Secret (The law of attraction). My life has changed a lot since I started following these principles. Joining this workshop by Vikas Trivedi was a turning point in my life. It has changed my view towards life. I feel much better and focused more than I used to do before. I love the way it has changed my attitude. Previously I used to get a lot more attached towards things which resulted in non-fulfilment of desires. Detachment from these desires has made me stable and I see things moving towards me. My wishes get fulfilled the way I want. If I focus on a thing the universe draws it towards me, be it people, things or whatever you want in your life. I feel the universe is synchronised with my thoughts. I have started working as an online seller of products, be it watches, handbags, clothing, footwear etc. and I am doing great in my business. Even I also saw terrific changes in my life and business partners. I can feel abundance and prosperity increasing day by day in my life, every day I am feeling better and better. I loved the session "Attracting abundance and wealth" which is being used by me daily. My heartfelt gratitude to my mentors Karen ma'am, Rosie ma'am, Hiral ma'am,

Dr. Nora ma'am. Pet El Rosch ma'am, Chloe ma'am, Vansessa ma'am, Maureen ma'am and my beloved brother and mentor Vikas Trivedi (Vikku).
Thank you so much!

Mrs. Kavita Sangtani
Jaipur, Rajasthan

CHAPTER FOURTEEN

FORGET THE PAST AND MAKE A MOVE AHEAD

I, Maureen Messier considered myself lucky to share my personal experience in this chapter.

I was what you'd call an early bloomer. By the time I was 16, I was speaking before crowds of 2500 people, as a result of involvement with Kiwanis International. Most weekends during my last two years of high school, I traveled the state of New York with a team holding workshops and conferences for the local teen clubs. After college I went to work in the fashion industry and poured myself into my career.

Life was good, but by my late 20s I had developed an unexplained anxiety. During this time I had gained almost 75 pounds in three months' time. The doctors could find no medical reason. Also, I was **not** overeating. At the time, the connection between one's emotions and one's weight was not widely thought about.

Shortly after, I had a *breakdown* where the repressed memories of my childhood sexual abuse came to the surface. After a few years, I was over my depression and over the trauma. Or so I thought. As I tried to piece my life back together, I found myself bound by irrational fears, procrastination, and other self-sabotaging behaviours.

Much of the shame I was experiencing wasn't from the sexual trauma. It was from the weight gain. I came from an industry where image is everything. I had tied my self-image to my physical appearance. So I became an expert at the art of wearing masks. The *good* church lady mask. The super mom mask. The victim mask. The untouchable bitch mask. The perfect family mask. The positive, enlightened person mask. Give me a situation; I could put on the mask. It was like changing fashion accessories.

What Lies Beneath

"You're an overcomer. Stay in the fight till the final round."

~ Mandissa, from the song Overcomer ~

The problem with masks is that when you wear them for too long you forget who you are. I embraced personal growth materials, including principles found in the law of attraction. Things were moving forward, slowly.

I had received plenty of great opportunities, but every time I'd start to experience success, I'd sabotage myself. I lived in a vicious cycle of hope, personal growth, action, fear, self-sabotage. I was stubborn though, because I never gave up hope. I just played small with my life, because playing big would mean removing the masks. Although I wasn't yet ready to move the masks, I was making big plans for when I would be ready to move forward.

If you cover up or deny your emotions, they lie beneath the surface of your life to fester and infect everything you do. You have to bring your emotions into the light for healing and then give them the proper place in your past and move forward. That's what brought me to…

The Day You've Had Enough

I remember the day I had enough. August 18, 2016 was one of those hot, lazy days of summer. I was in bed, bemoaning the state of my life. I had had a great recovery from a life threatening illness, only to catch a systemic infection. I was bedridden and miserable. Emotional and angry, I kept thinking, "How could I have come so far and have it all snatched from me now?"

As I was on my bed crying, I replayed my life- the joys, the regrets, the what ifs. I desperately wanted the chance to start over. I was not going to go down without a fight. A good friend suggested a liver cleanse, I decided to start there. I had nowhere to go but up.

The Unboxing

My box of liver cleansing ingredients arrived the next day. Within the first 24 hours I lost 18.1 pounds of toxic water weight and was feeling much better. That gave me the strength and clarity to tackle what really needed to be unboxed.

I decided I was going to stop playing small. I would no longer play the victim in this drama I co-created. I was ready to put on my big girl pants and **do** the hard work. It turns out the work for me was not as bad as I thought it would be.

As I pulled out what was in my box, I eagerly took notes. This time nothing would be left to chance. I wanted permanent change. What's in the box is different for everyone, but can be broken down into these categories: my limiting beliefs, stories of my past, and a hopeless view of the future. These are the things that hold you prisoner. Your fears and self-sabotaging behaviours all stem from these root causes. For years I had been working on eliminating those behaviours, now I was just going to go ruthlessly for the root.

So, into my notebook I created my first seven pages:

- **What have been my limiting beliefs? -** Which I immediately released through EFT.

- **Loving Myself Madly** - These are the gifts, talents, and other things I like about myself. Each one begins "I am_____." I also said these out loud in front of a mirror.
- **Everything I Want** - This is where I wrote all the dreams and hopes I still had for myself.
- **How has my pain and suffering moulded and shaped me for the highest good?** - This is where the seeds to destiny are sown. Your mess can be your message.
- **What has living in bondage to my past cost me?** Answering this question was the most painful for me.
- **What is no longer serving me?**
- **How can I show up for myself and reclaim my voice?** How I can start treating myself with respect and how I want to impact the world.

I believe this worked for me because I went right for the root causes of my bondage. I was willing to uncover what was lurking beneath the surface. I was finally brave enough to put down the mask and be vulnerable. Even though it would be hard for me, I knew had to be open to receiving help, increase, blessing and love.

I was being changed from the inside out as if by a power not my own. Once I started this process, there was no going back. I was being fuelled by the intense desire to restart my life and the emotional storm within.

It was not easy. I had critics surrounding me, upset with the changes they were seeing in me. Instead of fighting with them, I realised that we were operating at different vibrational frequencies now. My sons were wonderfully supportive; however, I decided I shouldn't rely on others for emotional mojo. I needed to be my own cheerleader and create my own support system.

Three Steps Forward, Zero Steps Back

"Every day I fight for all my future somethings."

~ Natashia Beddingfield from the song Strip Me ~

To create a system that would support me during my metamorphosis, I expanded the concept of my notebook. This would be my guide book, my planner, and my vision. I left nothing to chance.

Own your life like a boss.

The second section of my notebook, is all about taking charge of my life. It's full of the masculine energy that gets stuff done and keeps you on track. It's the strategic plan for how I can show up for myself. It's all about creating powerful systems for me to be responsible and productive, allowing me to reclaim my life and create the lasting prosperity and success that I deeply desire. This section of my notebook includes:

1. What is success for me?
2. Ways to honour and support my *new* self.
3. An honest evaluation of my current state in these areas: finances, time management, home management, health and body care, personal care and grooming, and systems and routines.

Each area has at least one page for goals and plans. I also address any fears, guilt or shame I had from neglecting these responsibilities. I look for the root cause and quickly counter with EFT and affirmations.

Intentionally create your life like a work of art.

The third and final section of my notebook is where I create living visions for every area of my life. These are written in the present tense and are sensual, describing my vision using all of my senses. This is what

I want to manifest. I frame every page with the concept "my life is a work of art." Here are my topics:
- My relationship with myself is a work of art.
- My relationship with others is a work of art.
- My body is a work of art.
- My lifestyle is a work of art.
- My appearance is a work of art.
- My Home is a work of art.
- My impact on the world is a work of art.

I will frequently envision my words in the morning before I fully wake, allowing myself to really experience what I desire. It's a daydream type state where I use all my senses and allow myself to *feel* what I desire to manifest. This has worked particularly well for changing the shape of my body.

Koi jaadu hone ko hai….so you better get ready!

Koi jaadu hone ko hai is Hindi for some magic is going to happen. I learned this concept from the Bollywood movie Bang! Bang! The main character tells the female lead about the concept of *one day*. Instead of saying, *someday I'll do* …, he lives his life as if today was that *one day*. He gives her the challenge to start doing the same. After looking death in the face, this really resonated with me. We are not guaranteed tomorrow, we have to like every day as if it may be our last.

I decided to reframe the expression a bit. By changing the meaning from *is going to happen* to *it **is** happening* puts everything in the present tense. For someone like me who had a real problem with procrastination, this subtle shift was a game changer. This is what I consider my *secret sauce*.

This is a very powerful concept to get you unstuck. If you view things as happening now, you are much more likely to get yourself ready to experience it. You begin to create the space to receive. You get rid of physical and mental clutter. You take care of your emotional baggage so you are ready for real love. You get everything into place so you can take advantage when opportunity knocks.

What I am sharing with you here is a perfect example. When Vikas asked me to write something for this book, I was ecstatic. With a two day deadline, however, I began to go into panic mode. I realised that I didn't need to worry because I had my notebook!

Once you are ready, that's when the magic happens.

Moving Ahead With the Magician
"Everybody knows I've got the magic in me"

~ Rivers Cuomo from the song Magic ~

If *koi jaadu hone ko hai* is my secret sauce, what I am about to share with you is my energy drink/rocket fuel.

The responsibility for creating the *magic* in my life rests with me.

This was a big realisation for me. I'd always wanted to create magic *with* people. That is a problem. The magic is within every one. With that burst of nitric oxide at birth, every human is endowed with their own unique magic or spark. It is up to me to bring forth my own light, my own unique expression to the world. Once I accepted this, things started to change in my relationships. I became aware of when energies needed to be changed and I adjusted *my* energy. Over time this has become more automatic, creating what seems like more authentic magical connections in my relationships.

Harness the moon to create magic plans.

A post about a new moon ritual came across my news feed in Facebook. It seemed interesting, so I decided to research the concept. Although it may seem strange, new moon rituals can be found in many ancient cultures and is even found in the Bible. If you accept the concept that everything has a vibrational frequency, this would include planets, stars, and moons too.

So in September 2016 I began what has become a *monthly moon ritual*. On the new moon and the full moon of each month, I write out everything that is not serving me. I also write out my intentions for the future, concentrating on the energies specific to that moon cycle.

At the appropriate time I go outside and burn the list of what is not serving me and read aloud my list of intentions. Whether it's the moon itself or the principle of the law of attraction at work, I cannot say for sure. I do know it works.

Approach life with a sense of wonder.
A major obstacle I faced during my transformation was the frequent cries of people around me that just wanted me to grow old gracefully, to accept that my time for doing big things was over. My philosophy has always been that it's never too late and you're never too old. I think this is what kept me going and fighting all these years.

I didn't go through this process to continue playing small. I try to look at every day as holding something magical for me to experience. I start my day thinking that today is a divine appointment. So I try to add as much fun to the mundane as possible. I look for ways to have more fun, more love, more impact. I schedule opportunities for growth, although God has unexpected ways for that to happen as well. It's amazing how changing your perspective can add so much value to your life.

It has been nine months to the day that I started this quest. It's been an amazing ride. Has it been easy? No, but I wasn't asking for easy. I was asking for lasting. Is everything perfect? Have all my intentions come to fruition? No. I am well on my way. I have my health back. I've lost more than 70 lbs. My business is back on track and moving forward. I am connecting with people on a deeper level now.

The most important changes, however, are on the inside. I am happy - truly, deeply happy. I have a confidence I have not experienced in years. I am facing my fears and messes head on instead of avoiding them. People that see the new me, don't recognise me. It's not just the weight loss, it's the glow from within.

****

REAL PEOPLE, REAL STORIES

First of all, I would like to thank you all mentors for changing my life and my thoughts process. Now life is more beautiful and easy. I always wonder that I am a capable to have the best in my life but always settle myself with less or compromised. The reason was no where outside. It was me only, who was earlier not able to recognise the fault within myself. I was rather finding fault in others. I am thankful to God that I came across to the people like you (Vikas and our mentors) who are helping others. After being associated with you, I realised that it is me only who is standing in front of my success. From you I have learned how, what and why should I do? After reading the books that you used to share with us, I realised where I was wrong! Thank you so much Vikku and all the mentors for opening my eyes and helping me in taking me on the right direction. I have become more down to earth person but my positivity has become higher and aiming so higher now.

Thank you all!

Naresh Singh
New Delhi, India

Hello dear friends! I was fortunate to be a part of the workshop which was held by Vikas Trivedi and all the international mentors. I am athlete so I need to have more positivity towards my goal. Vikas's one of the session touched my heart was "the law of echo". By using that I have won many gold and silver medals. I loved one more session by Karen about "Mirror Talking". Rosie ma'am explained in her session about "The law of attraction" . Today whatever I am, I give credit to Vikas and all the mentors. Vikas (Vikku) has a great knowledge about Psychology, once he said, "Energy and lethargy both are your opinions not your physical reactions". I tell you literary that sentence took place in my mind. And I got busy in winning more marathons and making money. I am living my life the way I want. I never get tired. Age is just a number; you must have a young thought and heart. I am blessed by all the mentors and Vikas has become one of my best friend in my life.

        Gratitude and love!

Shweta Shah
Pune, Maharashtra

CHAPTER FIFTEEN

Karma:
The Law of Nature

Nine-year-olds Jake and Billy walked to school every morning. One day, they passed by a beggar in ragged clothes and messy hair, who held up a cup and said, "Some alms for a poor old man, boys? I haven't eaten in days." Billy walked up to him and in one swift motion slapped the cup out of his hand and ran away laughing as coins fell to the floor. Jake who is very kind, walked up to the beggar and helped him pick the change. Jake felt bad for the beggar and took twenty rupees from his lunch money and gave it to him. "God bless you child," the beggar said as Jake walked away.

The beggar bought a loaf of bread and a bottle of water with his money and walked towards the park to feast. As he passed by, he saw a traffic cop slogging in the sun, sweating and looking parched. The beggar remembered Jake's kindness and decided to be kind too. He walked up to the cop and handed over the bottle of water. The policeman thanked the beggar and downed the entire bottle thanking God for the Angel he had sent.

Once the policeman finished his work, he got on his bike and left for home. On his way, he noticed a woman on the road trying to start her scooter in vain, while vehicles behind her kept honking and abusing.

He suddenly remembered how kind the beggar had been and decided to show some kindness himself. He stopped his bike, walked to the lady and diverted traffic away from her. He then helped her start the scooter. She was so overwhelmed by this man's kindness, that she invited him for dinner to her house, with her family, so she could repay his kindness.

That evening, the policeman, the mother and her son sat down for dinner. "What's your name young man?" the policeman asked the boy. "It's Jake, sir." He replied.

Just as the policeman was about to leave, it began raining, heavily. The policeman decided to take a cab home and come back the next day for his bike.

While the neighbourhood was deep in sleep, a band of thieves lurked around. They had targeted Jake's house, knowing the father was away on business and only the boy and woman lived there. As they approached, they noticed the police bike in the driveway and panicked. "A policeman lives here too!" they said. They decided to leave the house alone and rob the next house instead.

The next morning while Jake and Billy walked to school, Jake noticed Billy crying. "What happened, Billy?" he enquired. "Jake, my house got robbed last night, and the robbers took all my toys and everything from my house."

Moral: What goes around comes back around. Do good, and good will be done to you, do bad and Karma will return the favour.

What is Karma? We've all heard of it, the law of Karma. Here's a little history about Karma: Karma translated from Sanskrit, means 'Action'. It has been referred to by many names and phrases over the years. In the Bible, Jesus says '*as you sow, so you reap*', meaning whatever happens in your life is the direct consequence of your actions. Science believes '*every action has an equal and opposite reaction*'. Buddha says, '*Karma is action, and Vipaka, fruit or result, is its reaction.*'

Something that devout religionists, scientists and philosophers all believe in is that your destiny is a result of your present actions. That every action you make now will yield some sort of repercussion in the future.

Yes yes I know about Karma but why should I waste my time reading about it? How does it help me?

Reverse the definition of Karma, and suddenly you have a life hack that will definitely make all your dreams come true. All your goals will be accomplished. So every action has an equal and opposite reaction right? This means every reaction comes from only your actions. This means your future can be designed by you!

What the law of Karma tells you, is that you can take control of your destiny, by taking control of today's actions. This is a wonderful revelation, because it means you can achieve whatever you want in your life, become anything you wish tomorrow, just by taking the right actions today.

How does Karma work?

Karma is a force, an energy. It cannot be explained, just like god cannot be seen. But Karma has been felt in action. So how do you make Karma work positively for you? Well it is simple. Positive actions will yield positive results. Negative actions will yield negative results. Giving alms to someone in need today will maybe lead to you winning the lottery another day. Stealing from someone may lead to you losing all your possessions in a fire. These are examples, but you get the point.

Sometimes wrong actions feel good and give immediate gratification. Beating someone up might make you feel stronger or stealing someone's wallet might make you feel richer, but remember, all your actions effect your Karma, your energy. As you do negative actions, your Karma takes on a negative form and soon enough, it all comes crashing down. So don't take wrong actions in the pursuit of immediate gratification.

Exercise:

Answer these questions and you will understand how to use Karma to your advantage. Be free and truthful, no one will see these answers but you.

Q. What have I done recently that has had a negative effect on my Karma? I have not received the punishment of my actions yet but the action I did

The Hidden Spark

was wrong. Example: *I kicked a dog who meant no harm to me. I did not pay the money I owed. I promised to help a friend but I didn't. I cheated a person who trusted me*, etc.

A. _____

Q. Can my action be undone?

Example for Yes: The friend still needs help. The money can still be repaid.

Example for No: The dog cannot be un-kicked

A. _____

If your answer is Yes, go ahead and fix the wrong you did. If it is No:

Q. What else can I do to correct my wrongdoing? Example: Apologise to the person you cheated and help them with a different problem. Find the beggar you shoed away and donate some clothes.

A._____

Now that your Karma and conscience is clean, you can focus freely on achieving your dreams, and Karma will keep coming back to help you and add a positive dose in your life.

Something To Always Remember About Karma

The effects of Karma are 'felt' not 'seen'. Just like our story above, you may not realise that helping a beggar will save you from thieves. You may never even know Karma helped improve your life. But believe me, it is in action, and like Jake in our story, you just have to do good and leave the rest to Karma.

****

REAL PEOPLE, REAL STORIES

Vikas sir used to always post aboutvery helpful topics and, I expressed my desire to join the workshop. I joined this wonderful workshop. Thank you universe, for introducing me to this workshop of divine angels of love who gave an awesome turning point to my life. After joining this group, never felt any lacking in terms of finance, relationships, health and in my work place. I have started savouring the unconditional love of the planet. I do not have enough words to thank the mentors, for their selfless love, kindness and mercy. Each and every word we receive from them is taking us to the mesmerising world, where we can get anything and everything we wish by changing thought pattern. The mentors shed light on many wonderful books and explained the crux of the books to us which are life changing are my favourite books. I convey my heartfelt gratitude and love to all the mentors who are spreading their divine love to mankind. Abundance cheque is a very nice gift and it works wonders. I wish many more people from all over the universe should benefit from this workshop. The main lesson I learnt from this lovely group is GRATITUDE which works like a magic wand. From the day this workshop started, my day begins with millions of thanks to the universe. I am reaping the benefits to which I am very grateful.

THANK YOU, THANK YOU, THANK YOU!

Sandhya H.V.
Mysore, Karnataka

 Namaste! I have a long story to tell you about myself because I have been through the worst time and situations in my life. But I only want to tell you my achievements through this superb book. I have seen poverty in my life so I know very well the importance of education and money in my life. But the important thing to utilise all your education and money in the right direction because a simple minor mistake can ruin you. I am an ordinary teacher who believed in living a simple life but I saw more worlds when I came in contact with this amazing workshop by Vikas Trivedi and his international mentors. I started taking dance and drama classes. I started focusing on my hobbies and paid attention to where exactly I am going? Simply I utter that I did not know that I was the engineer of my life but after listening to the mentors and Vikas, I took the command of my life. I love myself. I love to live now. I have become rich by my soul, spirit, mind, heart and body. Thank you tons of times to all the great mentors.
Gratitude!!

Ami Patel
Surat, Gujarat

CHAPTER SIXTEEN

SWITCH WORDS

"Belief and intension are paramount for Switchwords to work."

~ Amanda J. Evans ~

The mind is a complex maze and its power has baffled scientists and psychologists for centuries. Through the proper use of the mind's energy, a person can bring about great change in his or her life. A large part of this power lies in the proper use of the subconscious mind.

The Subconscious Mind

Your conscious mind is what you use actively, to analyse situations and come to logical conclusions, to perform activities, to read, etc. The subconscious mind is one that sits in the background collecting memories, thoughts and feelings to reuse in the future. As a grown up, have you ever eaten a chocolate and suddenly felt nostalgic about your childhood? Have you heard a song and suddenly felt elated? All these feelings come from the subconscious mind. When you were a child, you had a favourite chocolate and eating it made you happy. Although it was just a fleeting feeling, your subconscious saved it and linked the flavour to happiness. The same way a song that was played at your wedding made you happy that day and you probably forgot about it the moment the song ended but your subconscious mind saved your state of positive energy and happiness, bringing it back every time the song is played. The taste of the chocolate and tune of the song act as triggers to bring back memories lodged in the subconscious mind.

What Are Switchwords?

Sigmund Freud understood this power and introduced the concept of Switchwords, which James T. Mangan later studied and theorized. Switchwords are simply words aimed at triggering the subconscious mind to induce a desired state of mind, the same way the chocolate or song did. Switchwords are powerful words or combination of words that speak directly to the person's subconscious mind. It might not make sense to the active or conscious mind, and might seem silly to few people but this is because the effect it has on the subconscious is not immediately visible. But to know the real power of the subconscious, you must first believe in the power of the subconscious.

In the book 'The Secret' author Rhonda Byrne talks about how the subconscious mind has the power to make changes in the physical world. For example, a person who constantly says they are unlucky forces the subconscious mind to believe this. The subconscious mind has the power to project this thought into the universe and before you know it, your car will break down. By convincing your subconscious mind that you deserve a lot of money, you can actually cause the mind to project this desire to the universe and you will 'attract' opportunities that will make you rich.

Now if the subconscious mind is this powerful, having control over it would make us extremely powerful, right? That is exactly what Switchwords do. They reinforce the beliefs of the subconscious mind and change the person's state of energy.

There are some universal Switchwords that work on anyone, for example the word 'COUNT' is used to attract wealth because everyone subconsciously relates the word count to counting money. There can also be personal Switchwords, words that work on individual people because of their connection to it. In essence, any word can be a Switchword.

For example, you might be an early riser who likes to drink a cup of coffee and watch the sunrise. Now anytime you're sad, chanting the word 'sunrise' will trigger the memory of sipping coffee and admiring the sunrise and instantly lift your mood.

Or if you're struggling with deadlines, using the Switchword 'DONE' reinforces the subconscious that the work is complete and before you know it, the work will be done.

How To Use Switchwords?

There are a couple of ways to use Switchwords. First identify what state of mind you want to be in and which Switchword will trigger that state. Then calm your mind and enter a relaxed state. Then you can chant the word out loud repeatedly, whisper it yourself, sing it, write it down or even think it. As long as you focus on the word, it will register in your subconscious. As you chant Switchwords, the subconscious looks for feelings and situations that the word relates to, and brings your body into that state.

Remember, some of these words might not make sense to your conscious mind. For example, the word 'CRISP' can be used to tell the subconscious to rid the body of fatigue and energize the person. As you chant 'CRISP' it won't make sense to you, how that word dispels fatigue but the subconscious relates to it and does the trick.

In your everyday life, look for situations that make you happy and then associate a word to it, preferably a word that was present at the situation. Chant that word and remember the situation that made you happy. Before you know it, the word will act like a trigger to bring about happiness whenever you're sad. Use this concept to attract not only happiness, but even tangible things like money and also people.

Here's a list of some Universal Switchwords:
ACT: become a better orator.
ATTENTION: Avoid mistakes and perform detailed work.
BAMBOO: Achieve rapid growth.
BLUFF: Eliminate fear; Improve imagination.
CARE: To memorize or retain information.

The Hidden Spark

DIVINE: Achieve extraordinary feats and receive miracles.
DO: dispel laziness.
FIGHT: Succeed in winning games.
GIGGLE: Get in mood for writing; enjoy current task.
HALFWAY: Make a long distance feel shorter.
INVEST: Increase devotion.
JUDGE: Improve comprehension; create love for reading.
KEY: Gain acceptance; access to authority.
LEARN: Feel and look youthful.
MASK: Shield from harm.
NOW: Stop procrastination.
OFF: Rid an unwanted habit; Fall asleep.
POINT: Increased focus; Improve eyesight; make decision.
QUIET: Silence the ego.
REACH: Find lost items; repair; recall.
SAVE: Stop affinity to alcohol and other bad habits.
THANKS: Free from guilt.
UP: Raise spirits and feel happy when down.
VICTORY: Achieve success.
WATCH: Learn or improve a skill.

You can begin using switch words right away. It is good to first get into a calm state. Try going somewhere silent and relaxing. Silence your mind and think of something happy. Now visualise what outcome you desire and the Switchword or combination of Switchwords to bring about that outcome. Begin reciting them a couple of times, sing them out or just think them. You don't need to spend more than 10 minutes. Proceed to spend the next 30 minutes doing something positive, that maintains your calm positive state. You can now chant the Switchwords throughout the day whenever convenient.

Energy Circles

If there's one thing Science and Spirituality agree on, it is that all matter in the Universe is made up of energy. Science calls this the 'String

Theory' and Spiritual Gurus, especially in India, call it 'Prana'. If you put yourself under a microscope you would see skin, then cells, then atoms, then electrons and finally pure vibrating energy. Everything in the Universe, and the Universe itself, at its core is made up of energy. In fact, not only tangible matter, even your thoughts are made up of energy!

Every person and object's energy interacts with each other and with the Universe by passing on vibrations. This interaction if a person's energy with the energy of the Universe gives rise to the 'Law of Attraction'. The 'Law of Attraction' has always been known, and was made popular in the book 'The Secret'. The concept is simple, if you have a thought in mind, the energy of that thought is passed on to the Universe. The Universe transfers this energy like a domino effect until your thought becomes a reality. For example, let's say you leave home with just 10 minutes left to catch a train. While you're in the cab, you keep thinking 'I'm going to be late, I'm going to miss my train, I'm going to be late'. This thought 'going to be late' is passed on to the Universe as energy and the Universe passes on this energy until all the traffic signals become red and your cab breaks down. Why? Because the energy you sent out was 'going to be late' and the Universe simply gave you what you asked for. You 'attracted' that outcome to yourself.

What Are Energy Circles

Now that you understand how energy works and how your thoughts can be passed on as energy to the Universe, let us talk about Energy Circles. Your thoughts can be in your mind, said out loud or even written down. All of these are equally effective and follow the laws of attraction by projecting the thought to the Universe, by way of vibrating energy. Energy Circles is a concept that says by writing down thoughts on paper and drawing a circle around it, you create a focus around that thought. The written thought now has more attention and focused energy that is radiated out into the Universe, thus making the attraction stronger. Energy Circles work best with Switchwords rather than vague thoughts, because switch words themselves have attractive power.

Using Energy Circles is extremely easy and extremely effective. It takes very little time but needs belief. There are some methods defined but a simple rule is to right down what you desire in simple text or by using Switchwords, draw a circle around it and then place the paper in a visible location. Because Switchwords work better than regular phrases, we will continue talking about Energy Circles using Switchwords.

How To Use Energy Circles
There are some rules that make the projected energy by an Energy Circle stronger. Firstly, you can add your name, or anyone's name to the top to improve focus of the Switchword to you or that person. Then, write down Switchwords that represent your desire or what you're looking to attract in your life. Do not use more than three Switchwords, because by adding more in one Energy Circle you dilute its power. You can use multiple Energy Circles instead. Finally, draw a circle around the entire text. It does not really have to be a perfect circle, but make sure the circle is complete with no open ends and is drawn in one motion. Make sure no text intersects the circle. You can even do this on a computer and print it out.

Here's an example:

Now paste this paper on your wall or place it on the table. The Energy Circle must always face up or forward or it will not work. Do not keep the paper at a location that moves a lot, like a drawer or a cupboard door and do not place it where it is hidden, like in a book. This dilutes its power and will not work. Studies have shown that using coloured text and circles, and adding concentric circles greatly strengthens the energy of the Switchword.

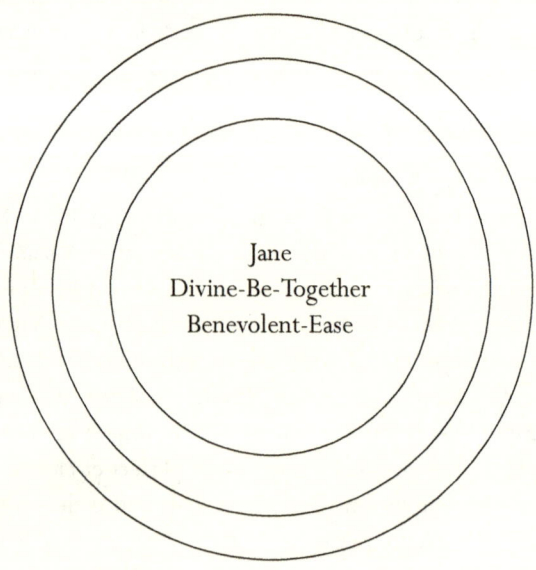

Finally, tearing up the sheet of paper releases the energy and stops projecting the Switchwords. You can use this to give a sudden boost in energy to the Universe before making a new Energy Circle, or when you have received your desired wish and no longer need projecting.

Just as specific Switchwords work in attracting specific energy, the colours of the circle sometimes have specific effect. A Yellow circle for example works on healing digestive issues or control problems. A Blue circle gives the person a relaxed effect, calming the person down. Gold circles help in bringing about a permanent change and Silver circles facilitate this change faster. Studies also show laminating the paper maintains the frequency of the projected energy by the Energy Circle. You can however work with a simple black and white Energy Circle and still receive all the benefits.

Energy Circles have known to have helped a lot of people. It is simple to create so you can try right away but remember, if you are sceptical of its powers and not sure it will work, you are projecting this doubt into the Universe and your wish will not come true. Your thoughts must believe you will receive your desire, then leave the rest to the Energy Circle.

"Switchwords have a tremendous energy to solve your solid commotions"

~ By the switchwords expert ~

****

REAL PEOPLE, REAL STORIES

I started getting success in my business from the beginning of this session. I have abundance of money in my life now which was not before. I never see the lack of money even I was separated from my family throughout this session I got lots big orders for my textile business and lots money success and by the healing of mentors your inspiring videos and lots love to dear Rosie, Karen and Dr.Nora. I have overcome my emotional trauma .I regain my self esteem and started to love myself and life. I do not know but I have become a magnet to money. All credit goes to the sessions and mentors. Thank you so much Vikas sir for conducting such a problem solving workshop.

Tons of thanks!

Simranpreet
Delhi

I am trying to practice the various suggestions provided by Vikas Trivedi and the workshop mentors in my life. I know eventually I will succeed extraordinarily. A million thanks for taking me as your student. You have provided study resources which may take more than a lifetime to study. You have provided more value through your course than all the exorbitant law of attraction courses put together. Your sessions are invaluable. I am short of words to express my gratitude to yourself and all the mentors. You are on a roll and God blesses you so that you can make a difference in more and more lives. I shall be with you along your success journey. One more thing, I loved your session "The law of you", now I take care of my words while speaking. I have become more soft and humble.

Thanks!

Manjumnath

CHAPTER SEVENTEEN —

AGE IS JUST A NUMBER

"Age is an issue of mind over matter. If you don't mind, it does not matter."

~ Mark Twain ~

The one thing that has killed more dreams than any other, is a person's age.

I have a friend who is one of the best guitarists I have ever seen or heard. When he picks up the acoustic guitar and finger picks, he immediately transports you to another calmer dimension. A few years back I lived with a roommate who would use charcoal to make the most enchanting portraits that you could stare for hours and not feel bored. A person whom I once worked with always wanted to code and build websites but she still continued to work at a meaningless job because she was afraid to quit.

To each of these talented people I had once said: "Wow you are brilliant! Why don't you just pursue this for life? It clearly makes you happy when you play/draw/code!" The three of them had the same answer:

I'm too old to start something new.

And those were the saddest lines I had ever heard. That was the first time I probably witnessed a string of words become a noose for dreams, and sadly it wasn't the last. I have heard many people lament when they reach their late twenties or early thirties 'I'm so old, my life is over'.

But I really fail to understand why! Yes, it is true that in most success stories we see on TV the lead person is a very young boy or a girl. What people need to understand is that, while this is an inspiration to youngsters, it is definitely not an ultimatum that only the young can make changes in their life that lead to success! Overtime this notion spread in society that all successful people start young and before we knew it, it became a rule.

There are innumerable examples in every stream of life: Art, Business, Music and Theatre, where men and women well past their thirties, forties, fifties and even past their seventies have made a drastic change in life to pursue their passion and become successful at it.

Sylvester Stallone is an actor who everyone knows. But what a lot of people don't know, is that before his most successful movie 'Rocky' was released, he led a life of extreme hardship. Sylvester Stallone first starred in a movie at the age of 25, which most people will say 'is a very old age'. But this was not even a feature film. He had a part that was shot in two days and he was paid $200 for it. He did it only because he was evicted from his home, was homeless and was running out of money for food. After another 5 years of immense struggle, at the age of 30, Sylvester Stallone said enough is enough, locked himself indoors for 20 days straight and wrote the entire script to Rocky. The rest is history.

There are hundreds of such examples, but I need just this one to convince you that age is only a number. What did Sylvester Stallone do different from my three friends I mentioned earlier? He did something any one of us can do: He dedicated his time and energy to his passion without worrying what his age was and what society deemed appropriate for a person his age. At the age of 25, he was homeless and out of money. He could have joined a hotel as a waiter or applied for jobs at a company but he didn't. At the age of 30, he ignored what society said and made his movie happen for himself, by writing the entire script. In fact, the story of Rocky itself is about a boxer who goes from rags to riches!

His story tells us three things. One is that you need to have a burning desire to pursue your passion. It cannot be something you try one day and abandon the next. It has to completely consume you. Second is that when you devote your time and energy to something you passionately desire, you become excellent at it. Third is that once you become excellent at something, the world will notice you and applaud you, without asking how old you are.

What would you do if the calendar was never invented? If there was no concept of hours, days, months and years? Wouldn't your perspective on life be very different? Sitting on your chair today you wouldn't know if you're 5 or 50. And if you wanted to learn a new hobby and make it a career, what factors would stop you? None I'm sure. Think about it for a second. Other than your age, is there anything at all stopping you from your passion?

I once met a married couple at a party and during our conversation the question of age came up. They laughed and told me that the woman was eleven years older than the man. "Didn't this worry you?" I asked them. This is what they told me:

"We met five years back at a friend's birthday party. We got to talking and quickly realized we were perfect for each other. I had a fixed job and was solidly grounded in my beliefs while she was a blogger and a free spirit. Opposites, I know, but our opposing lifestyle intrigued us. We kept meeting over the next few months and spent time together until one day we were madly in love. We decided to get married and on the day we went to get registered is when we realised there was an age difference of eleven years. We couldn't care less. We were so busy enjoying each other's company that the question of 'age' never came up".

This story of theirs really struck a chord with me. When you truly love someone or love doing something, age becomes irrelevant. The only thing that matters is if you believe you can commit to it, whether it is a passion a hobby or a relationship.

I want you to close the book after this chapter. You need some time for self realisation. Take a piece of paper and write down something, or everything that was once a burning passion in your life. It could be anything from writing a poem to becoming a rockstar, from becoming an entrepreneur to becoming a chef. It has to be something that once consumed you, that kept you up at night and forced you to wake up early, something that you once could not live without. Now close your eyes and imagine you have done it. Imagine you're on stage in front of a million people reciting your poem, performing a song, or giving a speech about how you started your million dollar company. Picture the scene clearly. How do you feel? Open your eyes but hang on to the feeling. That feeling of elation and accomplishment is how we must feel every single day. Now on another sheet of paper write how you're going to start and pursue that passion. Write down realistic goals and milestones and stick the paper on a spot you see every day, like your mirror and now start living the first day of the rest of your life.

"Age is just a number, maturity is a choice".

~ Harry Styles ~

****

REAL PEOPLE, REAL STORIES

How I identified the new in 'ME?

Each and every soul living on the earth yearns for love and to be connected with everyone forgetting that the soul himself/herself is pure love and light. The very purpose of the soul is to be happy and we on the other hand find infinite ways to be not happy. The thing that helped me most are the books (motivational and self-help books) and secondly, I decided whatever I see and whatever I come across, there should be positivity in it and it should help me grow, so I started searching groups of motivation and enrolled in it. I started practicing the art of gratitude. Do it until it becomes the second nature of you like, one day, I drank water and I simply thanked universe for the clean water which quenched my thirst unintentionally and I wondered how much deep I am into gratitude. Take control of your happiness and don't let it in other hands. Affirm yourself that you are born to be happy and joyful and no matter what happens you remain calm and peaceful. You may fail in the beginning but stick to it very firm and visualize and feel (daydream) a lot which makes you happier. Feel the goals of your life as if it happened already and you are a success. I learnt that hating or complaining about a person or situation would not help you; instead choose to move on, don't pay any thoughts to it if it is affecting you. Focus on the good and try to see the soul of the person who bothers you as souls are all helping and lovable; it may try to teach you something. In every situation, try to analyse it and be open to learn something instead of being emotional and of course be always thankful for the universe that it is helping you. I affirmed for my kid, when I was pregnant that he should be a successful entrepreneur and multibillionaire; now, I am into many businesses and feeling successful and happy. I am teaching him also to affirm and visualize. Start loving yourself more than anybody. You do not need anyone to love you always and make happy unless you discover that your love for yourself will make you whole. Everyone has an inner calling, so calm your mind and try to find it out. It will appear and your gut feelings know your life's purpose. Always, affirm and affirm and repeat it to yourself and one fine day, you will be feeling all your negative thoughts are vanished and continuous positive statement go repeated in your mind and that is the SUCCESS and live for the moment, NOW. As the same happened in my life, where I felt I am lonely, depressed, and frustrated; I repeated and affirmed all the positive statements and read all the powerful books to boost me up. I realized that it is all in me, it is me who choose to be happy or unhappy. We are left with two choices; either move on or dwell with negativity. Just be adventurous, give a shot, try to move on with positivity and you will find life gives you innumerous ways to be happy for. Every day as you *soon as you wake up affirm yourself that TODAY is the best day of my life and the universe is offering me unlimited abundance and I deserve the best. Believe me! Life loves you! Miracles do happen! Finally, I am very grateful and blessed to be part of Mr. Vikas Trivedi's motivational and brilliant workshop who does great service to the fellow beings with his mentors, Ms. Rosie, again; an angel in disguise with so much love and affection; and, Ms. Karen, excels in outstanding relaxing audios, which personally helped me a great deal and all mentors.*

Rathi Priya
Tamil Nadu

CHAPTER EIGHTEEN

IMAGINIOTIC THERAPY

"I am enough of an artist to draw freely upon my imagination. Imagination is more important than knowledge. Knowledge is limited. Imagination encircles the world."

~ Albert Einstein ~

Imaginiotic - means the place where you imagine freely. It does not require anything or cost something to imagine about your dreams. As I have told you in my previous chapters that you all are provided a great power to think or fancy about something. It does not cost anything. The law of attraction itself says that, "By thinking or feeling about your wishes, you attract them into your reality" When you imagine yourself attracting or being something or someone, you allow the law of attraction to work for you, it starts to bring into reality. Imaginiotic Therapy is also one of them which introduce the law of attraction in easier way. This therapy is a kind of process which includes the law of attraction, your dreams, the universe and this process.

If I say that there is a camera upon you and you are being captured by it everywhere or if I give to you the very life you wish to live, how will you feel?

Suppose, you wish to live in a beautiful world where you find the things wanted the most like good health, wealth, happiness, prosperity, life partner, suited opportunities, delighted family etc.

How will you feel? Of course, you will feel fantastic because you have had your beautiful world.

Here, imaginiotic Therapy also represents creating your own beautiful world the way you want.

You need to think about your dreams that what you exactly want in your life. Once you have decided on something to achieve in your life, then you will need to create your own beautiful world but that must be specific and a special place where you can live with your goals as if you have already received in your hand.

Imaginiotic Therapy means imagining the thing you want in your life in your own beautiful world, so that you can inhabit in another world. Select the aims from your list and plan them the way you wish to have in your life. Humans have been given the biggest power which is to attract something in your life by imagining in your life. Prepare your mind to create another world for you where you can see only those things that you want to behold there or you wish to possess there. Enter that world with your full faith and imagine yourself that you have already received everything and having in your hands. You are advised to meditate daily and visualise as if you have entered in your own world.

> *"Vision is the art of seeing things invisible."*
>
> ~ Jonathan Swift ~

Suppose, you wish to have a lot of money and prosperity in your life. Think about it, fix about the amount, wealth, bank balance, house etc you wish to have in your life. Collect some pictures from the internet — of money, currency notes, and houses, the places you wish to visit and look at them and try to capture those pictures in your mind. Place all pictures in your invisible world. Now it is time for you to meditate to attract all in your life. Live the life full of prosperity and wealth you wish for. Just imagine yourself as if you are in the real world. This will be followed by you until you get the same real world the way you want. Your vision must be clear that actually you are receiving the things you want to get. You have to be happy while meditating and feel happy. This is one of the unbeatable therapy which has been used by many attendants in my workshop including myself and received tremendous results. This process is called therapy as it is quite easy to create another world where you can live, talk, feel, create, imagine and bring these all into reality.

> *"Our imagination flies, we are its shadow on the earth."*
>
> ~ Vladimir Nabokov ~

If you put imagination and meditation together to fulfill your dreams then you can be a dream fulfiller. Your wish can only be away little from this therapy. In this practical book, you have already been introduced to meditation but here I am presenting the different technique which comes in Imaginiotic Therapy.

The way to use this therapy:-

- Sit in a meditation pose closing your eyes.
- Enter the world that you have created.
- Just feel as if you are seeing yourself in a state of mental peace, good health, wealth and abundance.
- Try to pull your attention at the center of your forehead and see the light there.
- Now, you have reached at the perfect stage of using the Imaginiotic Therapy.
- Press your Tragus (The tragus is a small pointed entrance of the external ears, situated just above the earlobe. It also is the name of hair growing at the entrance of the ear) inside of your ears with the help of your index finger gently to shut your ear

- The tiny veins of the Tragus is connected to your subconscious mind. By pressing the Tragus, you activate your frontal lobe, you activate your subconscious mind.
- You are advised to do this therapy everyday for 20 minutes any time.

Imaginiotic therapy does not only help to activate your subconscious mind but also helps you to get connected with the supreme universe and free yourself from inner and outer physical and mental issues.

You can begin your desired life anytime by using the Imaginiotic Therapy. You can begin it right now. Embrace the word now and flow with the present moment. You don't have to stop to think about the process as once you begin it, it starts to work for you because you have the power to create your own world.

REAL PEOPLE, REAL STORIES

Hiii! I have very good life by blessing a small but helpful family. I am so happy in my family. I had always desire to do something in my life especially in education field but I interrupted my study after marriage and had no chance to restart it. I got busy in my family and business. Luckily I heard about the workshop which was held by Vikas and some mentors. I requested him to make me a part of that workshop and was added to that group. Initially it was a bit difficult to understand but later on like magic happened. I started taking interest towards my study and I took admissions for my further study in the university. Vikas personally helped me a lot in completing my projects and study and motivated me for the best result. I changed my life very much and now I can say that yes! I am living my life. The entire credit goes to Vikas and his team.

Thank you!

Hilore Singhavi
Rajkot, gujarat

Namaste! I have lots of things to tell about the workshop. I must say that I started my life from zero. I have my beautiful family and everything is so fine but I wanted to do job in a big firm as well as on a big post. But the problem was that I had no such a big degree which was required. All I wanted was to get a good job. I joined the workshop where the mentors were guiding me the simple but powerful concept "Believe in yourself not in your degrees". Later on Vikas sir took the session about NLP which helped me a lot to get my job. I completed my masters degrees and I started applying for the job without thinking about my qualification. After a couple of months not only did I receive a good job in the college but also I started my own business which has made my life. The session "The law of Echo" motivated me too. I am living my life now with my dreams.

Thank you!

Sakshi Trivedi
Rajasthan, India

CHAPTER NINETEEN

I was Fool but Now I am Full

"Life is a dream for the wise, a game for the fool, a comedy for the rich, a tragedy for the poor".

~ Sholom Aleichem ~

If you go back to your childhood or some of your pasts' mistakes, you will find yourself guilty or call yourself a fool. It is a natural tendency to make mistakes to learn something new and experience of your life. Pain and problem, both are good teachers of your life but you always find it so difficult to face and that is why your problem becomes your pain in order to ignore it. If you ask me, the mind is a very astonishing thing, it makes or destroys you. It depends on you how you use it or how it uses you. Being a student of psychology, I read a lot about the mind before writing this book. I observed that human's mind is like non living thing which works like a machine in human's life but it has a very great and important role to play in your body. You get up in the morning and go to bed at night, in between you only do your job but you forget to focus on the activities you do. You forget to pay attention towards your thoughts that is why you never know the importance of your mind and you find it everything impossible. There is French proverb, "If your left hand has a problem, your right hand does already have a solution." The action part decides your life. Without taking actions towards your goals, you will remain empty. You take actions towards your goals when your mind is prepared because if your engine does not help you, you can't make a single move with your vehicle. I also found that the human's mind is pretty unadjustable or stubborn because it never accepts the new changes that your situation brings to it in present time. Your mind loves to hold the past things; it does not matter whether it is right or wrong, good or bad, positive or negative. It only likes to think about the past happenings which have already been taken place in your life because your mind is psychologically attached to things, events, accidents, or people known to you. It means that your mind loves your past but when it comes to present moment, it doesn't get ready to accept it . Why so? Because it doesn't like the new changes. Your mind is scared to have new changes. It panics to admit the present positive vibes. This reason is the essential one in your life that your past is holding you back or you want to do many great things in your life but you cannot do it due to lack of concentration and will power. That is not you, you are not at fault at all, and the credit goes to your mind and your thoughts, only.

The only thing you need to change is your mind — the way it looks the things and the steps you take towards your goals.

I had many attendees in my workshops. They initially thought themselves to be foolish people as they have indulged in many things like arguing, fighting, teasing, backbiting, stealing, being unsuccessful etc which they now know that they shouldn't have. What was important was what did they think now?

My message, especially to young people is to have courage to think differently, courage to invent, to travel the unexplored path, courage to discover the impossible and to conquer the problems and succeed. These are great qualities that they must work towards. This is my message to the young people.

~ A. P. J. Abdul Kalam ~

I am presenting here examples on basis of my sessions that how members used to tell me their stories and later on what were their words turned out to be?

Fool: I hate my job because no one admires me here and I feel lethargic.

Full: I will act upon my inner intuition and hobbies to create the desired work and focus on smart work.

Fool: I feel so sad when I cannot buy my dream house and my desired car.

Full: I have strong feelings that I have my own house. I visualise myself living in it and driving my own car.

Fool: I am so poor at studies and feel so inferior in front of others.

Full: I am the best version of myself and I am focusing on my strength to explore more to do something big.

Fool: I am from middle class and not so good looking that's why nobody wants to be my friend.

Full: I am the best version of myself. I have to believe in myself that I deserve the best. I have to accept myself to get myself accepted by others.

Fool: I feel frustrated and weak when my body does not help me.

Full: I am eating healthy food now which provides strength and stamina to my body, restart with renewed vigour. Healthy eating habit is part of my new lifestyle

Fool: I hate the place I am living in; it gives me negative energy that I will always remain poor.

Full: I can visualise my new home and I intend to live in it within some months.

Fool: I am sick of getting no result and success despite hard work.

Full: I attract each and every good thing to me. Failing in something teaches me to work smarter and not to just work hard.

Fool: I have some mental issues and family problems too.

Full: I mediate everyday and have fines vibration which make me more focused. I love my family.

The concept which is given here in "Fool and Full" actually it's just the difference between how you used to look at the things and how you see it now, the situation is same but the way you see the things that empowers you to stay focused and cool and brings you to your aims and other people are stuck there because they remain unknown to this secret.

"Every day you have plenty of opportunities to get angry, stressed or offended. But what you're doing when you indulge these negative emotions is giving something outside yourself power over your happiness. You can choose to not let little things upset you."

~ Joel Osteen ~

****

REAL PEOPLE, REAL STORIES

No one can change a negative person in one's life but the miracle breaks your myth. I did not believe in these all laws but I joined this session with no purpose as such. After one month I decided to use the LAW OF ATTRACTION once. And the teachings by the mentors made me attract 100,000/- effortlessly. Now the law of attraction has become part of my life. Vikas sir's attitude has touched my heart.

Thank you! Thank you! Thank you!

Bhausaheb Rajwade
Nashik, Maharashtra

Hello friends!! First of all I give huge thanks to all the mentors. You people have become my life to live. I was in need of a true person who could support me as a friend but I have received a true friend and younger brother, Vikas. I wanted to buy new mobile with 4g compatibility past 3-4 months but I couldn't afford it. Lately I started visualising somebody gifts me 4g handset. When I joined new office to my surprise I got new handset. Yes, of course it had 4g compatibility. My PF amount was pending almost 2 years after many follow ups. One day my mentor asked me to write Abundance cheque and I did it. Within 2 months I got my money. These 2 things back to back happened in my life which was not less than unexpected miracles. My life has become a beautiful priceless car and I am only the driver of my car which is being driven by me not by others. Thank you so much all of my mentors and my little brother Vikku (Vikas).

Preethu
Maharashtra

Chapter Twenty

Time Management (Dealing with Procrastination)

Once, Canadian-American businessman Elon Musk said, "I've actually not read any books on time management."

He is literally right but I thought of taking session upon "Time Management". The famous proverb states, "Time and tide waits for none". Yes, time can never get back but it can be utilised wisely. Today I reveal one secret of my life is that, I took two years to understand only two lines in my life which can be cliché for you but for me it was the biggest challenge to accept it and those two lines were — Believe in yourself and Use your time wisely. I know that you will be thinking that these both lines are known to you but believe me once you think about both lines again, you will find yourself unknown to both lines because you only know these lines but you don't apply in your life. Simply I took two years in applying these magical lines or the great qualities in my life. One bitter fact of your life is that you are not immortal, you belong to the earth and one day you have to leave everything here. Then what will be yours? The exact and true answer is 24 hours that you receive very day by the universe. Those 365 days that you receive in a year. What you do in meanwhile that decides your life. That sets your life. Once my teacher said, "You can please God by making a good use of your time." Actually the time you have that is the biggest gift by universe to you.

The word procrastination can be divided in two; "pro" meaning forward in Latin and "crastination" meaning belonging to tomorrow, together with the meaning "moving forward tomorrow." My mother had cultural quotes to refer to when teaching me life lessons; I remember she would say, "Don't leave for tomorrow what you can do today." In essence, my mother was teaching me not to procrastinate; which is a good parenting lesson. In my life, I have been guilty of procrastination many times before; it is a constant life battle that some of us face. Fear is the most common reason why I procrastinate; my fear of success, my fear of responsibility, my fear of failure, my fear of change, my fear of challenges and my fear of the unknown have all kept me procrastinating and deterring my goals for years. I ultimately needed to learn how I could confront my fears and carry on with my goals in a timely manner.

In order to accomplish our goals we must be willing to prioritise them and plan ahead; time management becomes an essential tool for our success. Dreams or as I like to call them "life goals" guide us in our path. Life goals can be external or internal. External life goals are the goals that are accomplished outside of us like owning a house or a car. Internal goals are the ones that are accomplished within ourselves; like losing weight and getting over an unhealthy relationship. Both external and internal goals will require effort, will require time, will require learning and will require us to believe in the beauty of our dreams. Our goals give us hope that we can become a better version of ourselves. In order to defeat procrastination one must be willing to identify our fears. One of the biggest fears in the human psyche is the fear of change. We are people of habits, rituals and routines; these keep us comfortable because we know what to expect. The fear of how change will impact our life, our relationships, our image, our job. We do not know what to expect from ourselves if we do indeed accomplish our goals. We may even fear our change will cause rejection from the people we love. We may fear losing our identity if we decide to change. The unknown can be very scary if we allow our mind to wonder far enough. The fear that we hold in regards to change can be altered if we decide to think about change in a different light, in a different perspective. Change is a positive thing when we are able to think optimistically about the future and ourselves. Think about the changes that have been positive in your life in the past and how change in those cases gave you a step forward. Our World changes every day; babies are born and people pass away every minute of the day. The flowers bloom and the weather changes day to day. Nature teaches us that we live in constant change and that we should expect change just like we do when the seasons change. We, ourselves, change physically, mentally and spiritually every day. When we were children we were excited about changes, you may remember being excited as a toddler when you learned you gained the ability to run. Toddlers become very excited when they discover their mobility. And as we know when little ones are learning to run they often fall. As adults we forget that falling is a normal part of the process of learning. Maybe you recall the change you experienced going into puberty. The physical change your body went through as well as the interest in getting to know more about your sexual organs that were changing. Perhaps you recall your first job and the change it required of your time and effort. Positive changes happen all the time, therefore, it is important to think about the positives that "change" brings into our life. If we are able to identify how change has impacted our life in a positive manner it will become easier to accept and honour. We may have never learned to honor change or even acknowledge it; it may be worth considering since it is part of the human experience. If we are able to think that the change we are undergoing will have a positive impact in our life we will be able to assimilate more easily to change and therefore fear it less and less. Confronting our fears is a stepping stone for confronting procrastination because it allows us to know how our thinking is sabotaging our goals. Another important factor to consider is our time management.

Time Management

Besides confronting our fears time management will become a great skill to defeat procrastination. Accomplishing our goals will require us to manage our time wisely and plan. In order for your time management skill to be effective, it must be done on a consistent basis. Managing your time will require you to schedule time to schedule your time.

Managing your life goals with the use of time management techniques can make you achieve your goals faster. I use the following P's to help me keep myself on task:

Plan — When we plan our time we are able to visualise where our time is being spent. We are then able to know how much time we can devote to a task. Familiarize yourself with timelines and use them to break the tasks of a goal into smaller steps. Using a calendar and writing your tasks along with the time you will devoting for each task can allow you to plan your time efficiently throughout your day, week and month.

Prioritize — In order to prioritise we must be able to know which step comes first in a goal. Goals that have multiple steps require us to identify the sequence of tasks that must be done in order to accomplish a goal. Once we have identified the sequence of steps and given them an order, a sequence or a number, (eg. Task 1, Task 2, Task 3) we can continue and start accomplishing the task at hand. Prioritising the most important task and accomplishing task by task will create progress throughout the development of the goal.

Punctuality —To have punctuality is to have due dates for your life goals. In order for a goal to flow smoothly we must set time limits. We need to know if the goal will be accomplished in an hour, a day, a week, a month. Setting realistic expectations and not under extending or overextending the time for your goal will create balance for your punctuality. Becoming punctual with yourself will take self-discipline, give yourself space and time for all of your goals within realistic time expectations.

Precision — This will require you to focus on the task at hand. The human mind has the tendency to wonder off when things get challenging, we can get distracted and not focus on our tasks. This is why we seek entertainment, to give ourselves a break, therefore when using this technique we must have the ability to redirect our focus to the precise goal or part of the goal we are seeking to accomplish. Precision is doing your best with the precise intention you set for yourself and not accepting anything other than your greatest effort and precision of your vision.

Power — To have power is to have the energy required to make the goal a reality. When one knows the power of their dreams and is certain that one has the power to accomplish our goals one becomes empowered to do what it takes to make the dream a reality. To have power can also mean to have a connection to a higher power that gives us faith in our vision and dreams. To have power is to know that we can accomplish what we think we can accomplish.

We live in a busy World and sometimes we tend to forget what we came to Earth to do, we forget about our passions and what drives us. Our journey can only be lead by our dreams if we allow ourselves to devote the time it takes to make them a reality. We must create a "cause" to be able to receive an "effect" and cause and effect can only take place if we take action. Procrastination is a dream eater; it will devour your dreams if you allow it to. Our fears are important to identify when we realise we are procrastinating on a goal. Many times fears paralyze us and don't allow us to expand to our full potential. When we are able to overcome that which we fear we can start the process of planning our goals and setting time to devote to their manifestation. Learning how to manage our time wisely is essential to the fruition of our dreams. When we dedicate time and space to our life goals they can bloom into reality. May the vision you hold for yourself not wait another minute; let us start making our dreams a reality today.

"The bad news is time flies and the good news is you are the pilot ."

~ Michael Altshuler ~

****

REAL PEOPLE, REAL STORIES

Success. Well, this word has a different meaning for me now thanks to the session organised by dear Vikas Trivedi (Vikku). As I remember, I found Secret in 2015 and started to apply it, but I still needed something more – go deeper and deeper.

Actually, I spent many hours searching and one day I found the info of this session.

I didn't win or earn a million yet; I don't run any business, but my success is my changed attitude towards many things. I feel this good energy now more than before. Actually, I attract and small things (like money, smiles, good people, recognition, etc.) in my life and that makes me happy.

Now I understand the meaning of the word GRATITUDE. And if something special happens in my life – I always say big thanks to the Universe and God.

Every time I look at the mirror I see a beautiful, awesome girl who can manage whatever. All that she has to do is — believe.

Finally, I want to say a special thanks to the mentor Rosie who helped me fight my inner demons – my emotions. God bless her. Thanks to Hiral for her numbers. It was like the drugs for me: overwhelming. I knew so many things; sometimes, it seemed that the mentors are reading me like a book — such similar situations and, honestly, such easy solutions.

Thank you for spreading peace to my heart; for healing me; for supporting and for showing that this world is so amazing and has so many cool challenges prepared for me. Rosie and Karen both are amazing personality and Vikku is so helping in nature.

Thank you so much!

ALINA,
Kelme, Lithuania

CHAPTER TWENTY ONE —

HIDDEN BENEFITS OF CRYSTAL

"Crystals are living beings at the beginning of creation"

~ *Nikola Tesla* ~

For centuries crystals have been used for their lucrative shine and aesthetics, moulded into jewellery and household ornaments. But what many don't know is that these crystals possess strong healing power. Yes, the exact same beautiful gems have the ability to alter energy and heal you, relieve stress and even attract wealth!

Crystal healing is holistic, non-invasive, vibrational energy-based healing. Everything in and around us is energy, and our ailments or negative impacts are a result of bad or misplaced energy. Crystals have the ability to absorb, focus, direct, detoxify, shift and diffuse energy. By placing specific crystals on specific parts of the body, negative energy can be removed from a person and their natural form of balanced energy can be restored.

Before I continue telling you about the methods and results, let me address the sceptics. So you don't believe a shiny piece of stone can emit vibrational energy that can alter our own energy? It's perfectly fine to doubt, that is what science is all about: doubt and solution. Ever heard

The Hidden Spark

of the piezoelectric effect? This phenomenon was seen way back in 1880. Crystals like Quartz, Topaz and Rochelle salt seemed to possess a unique ability. When mechanical pressure was applied on them, the emitted an electric charge! And conversely, when they were electrically charged they were seen to expand and contract. This phenomenon is being used today in voltage generators, sensors and motors.

Do you now believe a crystal is more than just an ornament?
Coming back to crystal therapy, finding the right crystal and method of use is the key to receiving full benefits. Different crystals interact with nature's electromagnetic forces and a body's natural energy differently, bringing about specific alterations and changes. Crystals can be used to calm the mind, heal, relieve stress, attract love and positivity, and even cleanse and align the chakras.

So how do you find the right crystal for you? There are two ways. If you know exactly what properties of the crystal you need, walk in to a gem store and ask an expert who will pick out the crystal for you. If you tell them *"I want a crystal to help me communicate better"* you will be given an Agate crystal and asked to wear it on you.

Another way to pick out a crystal is to simply let the crystal pick you. When at the gem store, close your eyes and focus on your inner energy, say a small prayer even. Then take your non-dominant hand and move it over the crystals. You will feel a subtle but noticeable tug from the crystal that you need. The tug might even come from more than one crystal. The tug is an indication of the crystal's energy interacting with yours, and that is the crystal you need. Finally, experiment by holding these crystals in your hand and getting a sense of how they affect you.

Great, now that you have your crystal, how exactly do you use it, or them? Again, there are a couple of methods. If you're looking for steady affect and benefits from the crystal, it is best to carry it with you. Some people carry it in a bag, but it is best to keep it closer to your skin, worn as a necklace or a ring. But they will still work if kept in a bag that is near you.

If you walk in to a meditation centre, they pick carefully chosen crystals and place them in specific geometric alignments on and around your body. These could be one hour sessions during which the crystals work to cleanse your energy, dispelling negative energy and strengthening the positive vibrations.

Another lesser known way to reap benefits of the crystals is through crystal elixirs. You can place one or more crystals directly into water, or place them in a bowl of water and dip a glass of water into this bowl and let it sit. Water absorbs the vibrations of the crystal, and you can then drink the water, taking in all the healing energy.

The beauty of Crystal therapy is that it is harmless, so in trying it you have nothing to lose. If you're thinking of getting a crystal but are unsure of which one, I've listed a few crystals and their properties to help you out.

Amethyst

Amethyst is an extremely powerful stone, mainly used for its protective aura. It safeguards against psychic attacks, electromagnetic stress and ill wishes and transmutes this negative energy into positive energy. Amethyst also has a calming effect, relieving the bearer of stress and anxiety bringing about a calming sensation.

In a physical sense, Amethyst is known to boost hormone production, tune the endocrine system and improve metabolism. It also cleanses blood and improves immunity, and is known to have a destructive force on tumours.

Rose Quartz

The crystal of love, literally. Rose Quartz is called the stone of universal love, and restores trust, love and harmony in a relationship. Rose Quartz purifies the heart and its desires, opening it up to promote love, self-love, friendship, deep inner healing and feelings of peace.

Rose Quartz also has a strong effect on the heart in a physical sense as well. It strengthens the heart muscle, improves blood circulation and purifies blood. It is also known to dispel chest, lung and kidney problems.

Clear Quartz

Known as the master healer, the Clear Quartz amplifies the energy of all other crystals and that of the bearer as well. It regulates your natural energy, by absorbing, storing and releasing it. Clear Quartz wards of negative energy around you and balances and revitalises the physical, mental, emotional and spiritual planes.

The Clear Quartz cleanses organs in the body and boosts immunity, bringing about balance in the body. It is also known to harmonize and align the chakras.

Citrine

Citrine is a crystal that brings about immense joy in your life, by energizing every level in life. Citrine attracts wealth, prosperity and success. It imparts joy, wonder, delight and enthusiasm, raises self-esteem and self-confidence. It also stimulates the brain, strengthening the intellect.

Citrine is also known to reverse degenerative disease and correct chemical imbalances in the body. Citrine helps correct eye problems, increases blood circulation, detoxifies the blood, activates the thymus, balances the thyroid and also relieves constipation and removes cellulite.

As I said before a crystal is non-invasive, and so it can cause no harm. But if you're still doubtful, I suggest going in to a meditation centre or a crystal spa. You don't need to buy the crystals, just use them through guided techniques. Once you experience the strong positive benefits, you will be running to a gem store to pick out your own crystal! And think about all the compliments the shiny new jewel will get you.

CHAPTER TWENTY TWO —

Your Problems, Our Expert Answers

(Answered by the experts)
QUERY 1. What is my purpose in life?
EXPERT ANSWER

1. I know sometimes we all feel the emptiness, the confusion, the lacking, and depression. We don't know the reason for this feeling and what should we do to change them? Our purpose is not happiness or success in life we need to know the reason why we are here. In other words, it's a way of thinking about what we want to achieve and how we can make sense of our life. Science has proved that the people who have purpose in their life, the better health and prosperous life they have.

    Our heart is the main source which can help us to find our true meaning and purpose. We need to question ourselves 'What truly inspires us?' 'What do we really love'? Then start taking steps in what we love to do, When we are inspired and happy, inspiration floods our heart and soul. I have different job titles. I'm a teacher, author, motivational speaker and a mentor. Each thing fills me with joy, happiness and energy but none of these are my purpose, they are my passions. We should get in touch with our passions.

QUERY 2. How to be a master over the mind?
EXPERT ANSWER

2. "Our life is the creation of our mind," according to Buddhist scripture. On an average we have 70,000 thoughts in a day and if our thoughts are unproductive then it can be the most destructive thing in our life. Our mind is very powerful tool and we need to use it wisely. The quality of our thoughts determines the quality of our lives. To master this, we need to reprogramme our mind as in chapter 3, "LEARN TO UNLEARN". We should choose our thoughts and then it will be able to reprogramme your mind with positive affirmations begin every day by saying yourself, "Every day, in every single way, I am getting better and better." Forget your past, stop thinking negative. It will seem to be hard at first but as you start focusing on your positivity.

   Be aware of your thoughts, you will find everything getting better and better because of new attitude towards life.

QUERY 3. How can I be hopeful when everything seems to be hopelessness?
EXPERT ANSWER

3. HOPE is directly related to our sense of possibility. It is the deepest emotion, happiness and optimism cannot exist without hope. It affects our mind and health it also affects the ability of a patient to get healed. Hope is actually something that we create, if we are going through bad phase in our life because of relationship issues, job issues, health issues soon, it shall pass as this is a cycle of life soon. You will be again basking in glory. If we shift our mindset from low emotions to high ones we can shift the entire balance of our life. I have learned that there are messages in our pain that can help our soul to grow. Hope is the life force that keeps us going and gives us something to live for. Being hopeful is

essential as it reduces our self doubt, anxiety, fear and stress as a result we have a higher level of self confidence and self belief and this will help us to overcome any situation in our life.

QUERY 4. Why is it so hard to let go off the past?
EXPERT ANSWER

4. We know letting go of past is tough whether it's our relationship or bad habits. But life gives us opportunity every day, every moment to create something new. I know it is easier to say than to do. The psychology tests reveal that it's our own resistance that we don't let go as change is always difficult at first, if once we make the shift lot of positive changes starts happening. Letting go of old attachment always opens up for new possibilities in life. We should understand that our past was only to make us learn life lesson unless we learn this. It will continue to happen. This acceptance brings calmness and relief and makes it easy to let go. We should celebrate our past that it happened and started practicing gratitude towards small things in life to make us feel content from inside. Keep yourself and your mind too occupied so not to dwell in past. You can get more idea on this from our chapter 15 "make a move ahead".

QUERY 5. Why we should practice gratitude in life?
EXPERT ANSWER

5. An attitude of gratitude in a simple term. Gratitude means thankfulness, counting our blessings and acknowledging simple pleasures in life. Gratitude shifts our focus from what our life lacks to abundance which is already present there. Psychological research shows that practicing gratitude affects our emotional, mental and physical well being in a positive way of practicing gratitude creates conscious awareness to think differently. Dr. Emmon says, "Saying that we feel grateful is not to say that everything in our lives is necessarily

great. It just means we are aware of our blessings." In order to start, we should do every day one minute morning gratitude session where we should be thankful to all the things in life, this will make our day better. Instead of criticising about others or our spouse we should show them gratitude for whatever good things they have done in our life this will make our relationship stronger and peaceful. In the movie The Secret we are aware of the law of attraction, it states that whatever we think or talk about will be drawn into our life and thinking about what we are grateful for will draw more of that to us. It's worth a try!!

> "Every day, think as you wake up, today I am fortunate to be alive, I have a precious human life, I am not going to waste it. I am going to use all my energies to develop myself, to expand my heart out to others; to achieve enlightenment for the benefit of all beings. I am going to have kind thoughts towards others, I am not going to get angry or think badly about others. I am going to benefit others as much as I can."

~ Dalai Lama ~

QUERY 6. How to overcome negative thinking habit ?
EXPERT ANSWER
6. "We don't see things as they are; we see them as we are." — Anais Nin.

Over-thinking or negative thinking is one of the major hurdles which we need to cross while working with the *law of attraction*. We know that what we focus upon we attract that whether its worry, fear or negative thinking. This drains our energy and makes us unproductive fills us with hopelessness so we must have ways to avoid this. First step is to know the importance of eliminating this and being aware of our thoughts.

When we catch ourselves thinking negative, we should switch over to positive thoughts and start visualising happiness and success. Start using positive affirmations saying affirmations on a daily basis as this reshapes our thinking, try making eye contact in the mirror when we recite them. Write all your negative emotions on a piece of paper, express all our pent up emotions in that paper and then burn this into ashes. If we are using more of negative words in our daily life then change those to positive phrases as this will change our way of thinking. Practice yoga because this shift our focus from thoughts to breathing this is very relaxing. Surround yourself with more positive people and practice the ritual of gratitude with each passing day if we follow this I am sure this will help you to break the pattern of negative thinking.

QUERY 7. Do you ever feel like you are going through life merely surviving rather than truly thriving?
EXPERT ANSWER

7. We are meant to be the creators of our lives. Anything we can dream about, we can create. We're not made to merely survive – we're made to thrive. Unknowingly many people are just surviving instead of thriving they have forgotten their goal or dreams in life and they are just living life in a routine way and I believe this can be the biggest regret in life living in survival mode. Whereas thriving can be so much more exciting as to grow to prosper or to flourish. just thinking about a life beyond surviving puts you closer to thriving. Creating a vision of your life and let it guide you, working towards vision will inspire you to take action. We should find out list of activities which you love to do passionately and spend time on these activities which help you build your mind, body and spiritual well being. We

constantly need to build ourselves, develop confidence by reading great books.

To create a vision board so it helps in to focus towards goals sticks inspirational quotes and pictures to inspire. Sometimes thriving is difficult than surviving because we need to break our habit and the resistance force within us but keep building yourself up and never doubt for a second that you are worth it.

QUERY 8. Do You Love Yourself?
EXPERT ANSWER

8. Many times people forget to love themselves. They have a question in their mind "What can I do to love myself"? Slowly you will discover to love yourself first, instead of loving the idea of other people loving you. By loving yourself everything starts improving in life – relationships, health, mental well being, self esteem etc. It's the key to love and create loving relationships with others. Loving yourself is important to create a passionate, fulfilled and joyful life. If we treat ourselves worthy of love, respect and compassion then our life will flow more effortlessly, abundantly, and joyfully. When you are chastising yourselves through negative self talk, judging yourselves. Criticising yourself is actually, you are paining yourself and that's the last place you want it to be. Disease starts way out in your aura and works inwards until it affects your physical body, eventually you become ill.

You can choose to stop your suffering. Start today by listening to yourself, how often do you praise yourself? Or tell yourself how amazing you are?

Learn to be self compassionate that means talking to yourself like you would talk to your best friend; choose to say different phrases like I am doing so well! Everyday I'm improving more! I love myself!

Look for the things that you love about yourself and gradually you will find more and more.

When you start to love yourself your life will reflect this out to the universe and the universe will reflect it back to you. The universe is really like a great big mirror what you say to yourself is mirrored straight back, so be sure that you always love yourself first.

QUERY 9. What limiting beliefs you are holding on to ?
EXPERT ANSWER

9. Many times we feel that there is more we can offer to the world but something hold us back like some invisible force. This invisible force is nothing but *you*; it's our fear, our inadequacy, our limiting beliefs, our negative attitude which holds us back from taking chances. It prevents us to accept gifts offered by universe as you are stuck focusing on the negative aspect of your circumstances. These limiting beliefs have a devastating impact on our lives as they are dominating they can control our thoughts, actions, and emotions as they are embedded deep inside in your unconscious level, so firstly we need to discover what our limiting beliefs are and start to look into our life. you need to make conscious choice by avoiding disempowering thoughts rather believe in thoughts which empower you with energy and desire. Then you need to act on these beliefs by making some changes and coming out from your comfort zone, but finding courage and taking action will be the biggest step taken it might be a painful process but you have to believe in your empowering thoughts.

"The only limits in our life are those we impose upon ourselves."

~ Bob Proctor ~

QUERY 10. How to get a matched mate in life?
EXPERT ANSWER

10. Many times it happens people are taken over by emotions, love, bliss and happiness, and are unable to think practically when taking decision to spend the life with one person and after few years the compatibility seems to be lost. As this is the major decision in life which holds our future so decision should not be based only on emotional being there are other factors also which need to be taken into consideration like common interest and hobbies you both share what are the expectations from each other and how much you can sacrifice willingly. Trust and relationship again is very important factor. Both are different individuals so you should learn each other's need.

QUERY 11. What do you want most out of life?
EXPERT ANSWER

11. The answer to this question never comes easy. Sometimes it takes a lifetime to figure out. We all want different things like success, money, relationships, wisdom and much more which can add meaning to life. First you need to find out what you are passionate about what u love doing more. The answer is hidden inside your heart look deep inside it will reveal you through longings, your desires, your dreams and whatever brings you the greatest joy. Listen to your truest self it will guide you. Great things never comes easy in life you need to take risk and accept uncertainty in your life to learn more sometimes it's the journey which is more fulfilling.

QUERY 12. Should we trust our intuition?
EXPERT ANSWER

12. "Your mind will answer most questions if you learn to relax and wait for the answer."

—William S. Burroughs

Intuition can be powerful asset to us assuming we should know how to listen to it, but most of the time we ignore it. Albert Einstein once said, "it is our most valuable asset, and one of our most unused senses". He described it as a feeling for the order lying behind the appearance of something. Sometimes it is referred to us as gut s, feeling, sixth sense, innate wisdom, inner sense, instinct, inner voice, spiritual guide etc. After meeting with a lot of famous people, I gather that they have made life's major decision on the basis of intuition. Intuition is the right navigating tool it is an alert to signs of changes and opportunities. Sometimes when we are in a situation, we feel depleted or exhausted this is a sign of a situation where you can become depressed, anxious or stuck.

When your intuition signals that you've found something or someone truly right for you, the choice often becomes strangely easy; It feels healthy, and good. There is no exact science which tells us how to listen to our intuition. Just clear your mind and heart and take a deep breath. Sometimes it is difficult to hear intuitive mind during distractions and troubled times. Be honest with yourself and acknowledge those unsettled feelings they are there to guide and support you. Listen to them.

QUERY 13. How should we feel about money ?
EXPERT ANSWER

13. Money is such an emotionally charged up subject we all want it but not willing to do things needed to create it. If we believe we don't have enough then there will never be enough, even there are loads around us. Ninety percent of people have negative feelings towards money when it comes to pay their bills, they feel frustrated, they curse it and every time they repeat it as in result money doesn't come to them it runs away from them. We need to celebrate money and take proper care of it as we know things taken care of lasts for decades. Whenever we are donating or giving money we should have right attitude of heart many of us feel pain after

giving as they feel they left with less. Sometimes we feel upset as we don't have enough to give but always remember we always have more enough to give, no matter how little if we have right attitude to give as then it will always multiply and get back to you.

Have positive feelings towards your money and you will begin to attract it. Continue to be angry or frustrated and it will forever elude you.

QUERY 14. How to stay healthy?
EXPERT ANSWER

14. Staying healthy is very important for physical and emotional well being as your body will be strong it will help you to cope with stress and also fight illness. Maintaining good health doesn't happen by accident. It requires work and smart lifestyle choices. First we need to eat right balanced diet rich in fiber, whole grains, fresh fruits and vegetables, "good" or unsaturated fats, and omega-3 fatty acids. Another important thing is to eat breakfast. Studies show that skipping breakfast triggers the body to eat more lately in the day and store calories. So we should eat smaller quantities in each of the three main meals with healthy, small intakes in between. If you eat more calories than you burn, usually you will gain weight as the body stores the excess. You're recommended to take at least half an hour of exercise every day. You can build exercise into your daily or weekly routine and get your friends involved too which will help to motivate you. It can greatly reduce your risk of heart disease, stroke, diabetes, depression it improves sleep and endurance. After eating right and exercising, you need to sleep. The average adult needs about eight hours of sleep per night. Sleep is the great cure-all. It is time when your body recovers, and when your immune system is improved.

Reduce stress is another strategy that can help you stay healthy, There are many ways to deal with stress, like meditation, mindfulness, and taking vacations.

QUERY 15. Is suffering caused by our karma or otherwise?
EXPERT ANSWER

15. "Do unto others as you would have them do unto you," and "What goes around, comes around" are common ways of talking about karma. Karma means the cause and effect of our thoughts and actions. Any physical or mental action is karma. Thinking is mental karma. Karma is the sum total of our acts, it means not only action, but also the result of an action. If there is an action, there must be a reaction. The reaction will be of equal force and of similar nature. Every thought, desire, imagination and sentiment causes reaction. It is the law of action and reaction that brings the fruits. Karma is not fixed and unalterable. Only the principle or "law" of karma is unalterable. You reap what you sow, we have our own karmic map. We also need to understand that each person has his own karma and acts according to it. The circumstances of our life occur because of our karma. It depends upon us how we deal with it positively or negatively. If we deal negatively and create sufferings for others the reaction will return to us in more intense form. On the other hand, if we do good and create happiness for others then it neutralises the karmic consequences gradually. We cannot control our fate but we can alter our reaction and in this way we cope with the burden of karma in any given incarnation.

QUERY 16. How can I work smarter instead harder?
EXPERT ANSWER

16. You can accomplish anything with hard work, but only working hard is not enough, you need the right tools, the

right strategies, for the right tasks. You need to work smarter, not harder. In other words, working smart essentially means figuring out what your strengths are and building a network around you to build upon those in order to reach goals in the quickest and most efficient way possible. Try to avoid multitasking because whenever we try to do lot of works in short span of time, we get frustrated by our lack of attention and reduced performance. You should avoid wasting time in phone calls and attending unnecessary meetings and make a list of things to do. Prepare a deadline for each set of task otherwise we might take long to finish it. Here "Time management" chapter plays a important role as you know managing time is not about squeezing as many tasks in a day it is about simplifying the work by identifying the most crucial task and to complete those first. Devote your entire focus to the task at hand. Concentrate on this one task. Nothing else should exist. Immerse yourself in it. Allow yourself to work in smaller chunks rather than sitting down to complete an entire project. Forcing yourself to complete the entire task will stress you out and make you less productive rather take a short break to keep your mind fresh and reduce your anxiety. That way, you can work to the very best of your ability.

QUERY 17. Why is it important to manage our time well?
EXPERT ANSWER

17. Our biggest problems are two - Procrastination (delay everything), and Over-thinking.

If you really want to make use of 24 hours then you must set a time table of your daily schedule.

Early in the morning will help you manage your time because it's in our hands to waste time or invest time. It seems that there is never enough time in the day. But, since we all get the same 24 hours, why is it that some people achieve so much

with their time than others? The answer lies in good time management. "Time management" refers to the way that you organise and plan how long you spend on specific activities. Benefits are enormous:
- Greater productivity and efficiency.
- A better professional reputation.
- Less stress.
- Increased opportunities for advancement.
- Greater opportunities to achieve important life and career goals.

QUERY 18. I sometimes fall asleep while meditation is that ok ?

EXPERT ANSWER

18. Falling asleep during meditation is very common. Perhaps happens with everyone once in a while. Slumber is associated with relaxation whenever we relax or our mind is silent we fall asleep. Sometimes people are not sleeping as much their body needs biologically so whenever they start meditating they tend to sleep. We may not notice our fatigue day to day So when we stop and tune in to our bodies in mindful meditation, we may discover that we are deeply tired. I would say to meditate first thing in the morning when you are most alert Choose an object of awareness, such as 'in' and 'out' of breathing. Always exercise before you meditate you can preferably sit outdoors to feel the breeze. Never meditate on your bed. Avoid eating a large meal before meditation. There is no "maximum time" for meditation. However, in any case, don't meditate longer than your motivation start with 15-20 minutes each day then gradually to 30 minutes. Simply follow the practice to the best of your ability. Keep your interest and your effort alive. Practice every day. This is enough for you to reap most of its benefits.

QUERY 19. How to pass in the examinations by using the law of attraction?
EXPERT ANSWER

19. Always remember "Knowing is not enough, but applying is important." Many people knew about the law of attraction but never apply its principles. I have come across several examples of students who passed their exams with 98 percent by applying LOA techniques as getting 60 percent was also unimaginable for them. At times, things don't go as per planning but if you are a believer of the Universe then have faith that the Universe has the best plan for you. The Universe doesn't work this way to give you everything without doing anything. Don't think Law of Attraction as a quick fix formula and just visualise for few days or weeks without studying and expect miracles. The Law of Attraction works in synchronisation with affirmative action. If you take action, study well and then you use the law of attraction, of course you will get miraculous results. Be confident and study happily however the big exams are, practice gratitude towards your teachers and feel grateful to everything related to exams even ID card, pens etc. spare some time in a day to relax and visualise the end result which you want for your exams. Close your eyes and see yourself jumping in joy and telling your family and friends about your desired score in exams and your pass result. Feel the joy of passing in your visualisation then open your eyes and feel good about your vision/your goal. Create a vision sheet or board and write your desired goal paste pictures relating to your goals, Every time you see it rather than getting doubtful and scared say "Thank You" and feel the happiness. This will program your sub-conscious mind to make you fully confident. You can also make a dummy mark sheet with same number of marks or percentage required and pastes it on a vision board It works like a miracle. I have seen many people who did this got the closest to result to this dummy result they prepared for.

****

REAL PEOPLE, REAL STORIES

I had just visualised that I am in Delhi on 25th February just to test whether visualisation works. Wow! it did really work. Oh my God! I was deputed to attend one of the workshops at Delhi from office. I had just imagined myself travelling through flight. It did happen the same as I visualised on 1st March, 2017.

Secondly, I had Samsung mobile which was old enough and was very slow to cope up with my daily activities on my android. Just I window shopped on my computer and visualized that I have a new version cell which can help me to read all the PDF books related to law of attraction. Wow! That too I got it. My brother-in-law gifted me LENOVO K6 POWER. It helps me a lot in reading the PDFs sent by our mentor Dr. Vikas.

Thirdly, I wanted to purchase a gold chain of my choice and I got that too.

These three back to back success stories happened continuously in the month of March, 2017.

I thank all the mentors for guiding us towards the richness in all aspects of life.

Thank You Mentors
ESPECIALLY DR. VIKAS TRIVEDI.
LOVE YOU ALL

Tejpriya
Bengaluru, India

Namaste, Vikas is like my son, but I must say that this boy has terrific knowledge about everything. I am blessed with everything in my so I never used these all techniques but yeah! Once Vikku had taken session upon Bhagwad Geeta which I loved it the most. The way he represented all the teachings was remarkable. A person who got himself enhanced spiritually then he no longer needs to be attached to this materialistic world but he balanced himself beautifully. I loved the one concept of that session that "Play to play not to play to win".

God bless you Vikas! And thank you so much all the mentors from the worldwide.

Neelakshi Chaturvedi
Ahmadabad, Gujarat

"Success is not a thing to be waited for; it is a thing to be achieved".

~ Smita Agarwal ~

"Change is the only Constant"

~ Shrimad Bhagwad Gita ~

www.ingramcontent.com/pod-product-compliance
Lightning Source LLC
Chambersburg PA
CBHW051649040426
42446CB00009B/1046